This book was written on the lands of the Gadigal people of the Eora Nation and the Widjabul Wia-bal people of the Bundjalung Nation. I pay my respects to their Elders past and present and acknowledge their deep, ongoing connection to Country, storytelling and culture.

For those who love design, who trust their instincts,
and who want their home to tell their story.
I hope this book is your permission slip -
the ingredient that brings it all together.

A VISUAL FEAST

JONO
FLEMING

INGREDIENTS
THAT MAKE A HOME

Smith Street Books

THE MENU

FIVE · LAYERS

161

Crafted Through Time

181

SIX · SPACE

199

A Quiet Revelation

219

SEVEN · CULTURE

233

A Bridge Between Worlds

253

EIGHT · STORY

267

Etched in Stone and Sea

285

DIGESTIVO

300

APERITIVO

Good design is a recipe for joy. A little light, a pinch of texture, a balance of colour and space, all blended to awaken the art of living beautifully. Much like cooking, design begins with knowing your ingredients, understanding their purpose and combining them in ways that feel just right.

My love for creating spaces began in childhood, in moments of quiet discovery. I'd lose myself in books, get swept up in paintings, linger over films long after the credits rolled, and marvel at the textures and colours of the world around me. I didn't realise it at the time, but those experiences were planting the seeds of a lifelong passion. They taught me that inspiration really is everywhere. It can be found in the way light filters through leaves, the weathered edges of an old book, or the warmth of a home-cooked meal. Each of these moments has the power to shape how we feel and how we live.

But passion alone isn't enough; it's the spark, not the shortcut. Like any skill, creating beautiful spaces takes curiosity, practice and a willingness to experiment. Over the years, I've learned that, at the heart of it all, lies connection – the relationships between objects and spaces, people and their surroundings, and the past and present. The best interiors tell stories. They reveal who we are, where we've been, and what we hold dear.

Understanding these relationships and telling these stories requires a blend of knowledge and instinct, both of which take time to develop. I first grasped this connection between instinct and craft, not in a design studio, but in a kitchen. My friend Silvia was teaching me how to make pasta. When I asked her how I would know when the dough was ready, she smiled and said, 'You'll just feel it.' Her answer frustrated me. I wanted specifics. But as I spent more time in her kitchen, I began to understand. It wasn't about following a strict measurement, it was about intuition, born from practice and observation. Eventually, I could tell when the dough was ready simply by feel.

It's the same with spaces. When a room feels off, your instincts are trying to tell you something. Maybe the light isn't quite right, the colours don't flow, or something isn't sitting right in the space. That feeling doesn't come out of nowhere – it's shaped by experience and an understanding of the basics. In the kitchen, you have to know your ingredients before you can trust your gut. Sometimes it's just a pinch of salt or a dash of pepper that will bring balance to a dish. In a room, it might be a shift in texture, a tweak to the layout, or bringing in more light. It's these little touches that bring harmony and balance, and create a space that feels right to you.

Instinct is deeply connected to personal taste. Taste is an extension of intuition, it's about trusting what feels right for you while allowing your preferences to grow and evolve. Just as your palate changes when you try new foods, your sense of style develops as you experiment and explore. We don't eat only one food forever, and our interiors shouldn't stay the same either. What feels right today might change tomorrow – that's part of the beauty. The more you lean into the process, the more confident and curious you will become about what resonates with you.

A big part of this process is learning to really look. Crafting a space isn't just about doing, it's about noticing. It's about the way textures play together, how light moves through a room, how a space invites you to pause or move. Paying close attention helps you understand the elements that work for you. It's a process of discovery.

The choices we make about what we bring into our homes matter. They shape how we live, how we feel and how our spaces

reflect us. Great interiors aren't just functional and beautiful, they are deeply personal. Every interior tells a story, and every story is built on key elements that bring it to life. Each detail, big or small, is an integral part of the atmosphere. It's not about perfection, it's about creating a space that feels like home and holds your stories, values and memories.

A Visual Feast: Ingredients That Make a Home is about creating spaces that resonate – spaces with purpose, beauty and heart. Each chapter focuses on one essential ingredient of design: light, colour, pattern, texture, layers, space, culture and story. Together, these elements form the foundation of every room, but how you mix them is entirely up to you. Make the recipe your own!

This book is a guide to crafting a home that feels personal, purposeful and alive with beauty and meaning. It offers inspiration, ideas and tools to help you bring your vision to life. But remember, it's not about rules or rigid formulas, it's about learning to see, feel and create in your own way.

More than anything, *A Visual Feast: Ingredients That Make a Home* is an invitation to slow down, look closer and trust yourself. Designing a space is like preparing a great meal – you are creating an experience to savour and share.

Jono

ONE

LIGHT

ONE

Light is to interiors what seasoning is to food. Too much is overpowering; too little, and the space falls flat. But the right amount enhances everything, bringing out depth, warmth and contrast. Just as a pinch of salt can transform a dish, the right lighting can completely change how a room feels.

‘Lighting is the poetry of architecture.’

LOUIS KAHN · 1901 — 1974 · ARCHITECT

Living in the Light

For years, I've lived in an apartment with limited natural light. The windows, although large, are at an angle that rarely allows sunlight to linger. Even on the brightest of days, the light feels fleeting, leaving long shadows in its wake.

I became obsessed with maximising every ray of sunlight that entered this space. I placed mirrors near the windows to bounce the light deeper into the room, I added reflective surfaces to stretch what little daylight I had, and I painted the walls in soft, airy tones. These small adjustments brought a glow to the space, but only on clear days.

When the skies turned grey, the apartment felt heavy, as if the walls were closing in. That's when I turned to lamp light. Carefully chosen table and floor lamps created pockets of warmth in the gloom. A soft glow in one corner, a reading light near the sofa, and the flicker of a candle on the dining table transformed the mood entirely. What started as a necessity became a ritual, a way to bring life to my home, regardless of the weather outside.

This experience taught me that light is more than illumination, it is the gentle embrace of a room. Light changes the way we feel, shaping our sense of comfort and connection. Thoughtfully curated lighting doesn't just brighten a space, it reveals its textures, highlights its details, and creates moments of intimacy and energy. Whether it streams naturally through a window or glows from a carefully placed lamp, light turns a house into a home.

Lighting is a powerful design tool. It is about more than just brightness or shadow, it's about the quality of the light, how it interacts with a room, its materials and its purpose. Light shapes the character of a space, painting it in tones of shadow and glow, and telling a story of comfort and connection. Learning to analyse the key characteristics of lighting will help you see a space clearly – not just how it looks, but how it feels.

DIRECTION PURPOSE QUALITY COLOUR TEMPERATURE INTERACTION

KEY CHARACTERISTICS OF LIGHT

① DIRECTION
Where is the light coming from? Is it streaming through a window, bouncing off a surface, or focused from above?

② PURPOSE
What is the light doing? Is it illuminating the entire room, highlighting an object, or creating a sense of intimacy in one area?

③ QUALITY
How does the light feel? Is it soft and diffused, casting gentle shadows, or is it sharp and direct, defining edges and textures?

④ COLOUR TEMPERATURE

Is the light warm and golden, cool and crisp, or neutral and balanced? How does it influence the overall tone and mood of the space?

⑤ INTERACTION

How does the light engage with the materials in the room? Does it enhance textures, deepen colours or create playful shadow patterns?

THE FOUNDATION: NATURAL LIGHT

Natural light is a transformative tool. It changes throughout the day, shifting a room's mood and energy. Spaces bathed in sunlight feel open and expansive, while those touched by softer, diffused light feel calm and reflective. Harnessing natural light isn't about controlling it, it's about appreciating how it changes throughout the day and working with it to enhance your space.

Start by observing how light interacts with your home. Notice which corners catch the brightest glow and which areas remain in shadow. Use this understanding to match the function of your rooms with the light they receive. A well-lit area might make an inspiring workspace, while a dimmer corner can be transformed into a cosy retreat.

For homes with limited natural light, reflective surfaces can amplify sunlight. A mirror placed opposite or adjacent to a window extends its reach. Polished finishes, like metallic accents or glass, can catch and reflect light, subtly brightening a room.

Natural light isn't just about brightness, it's about character. The gentle glow of early morning, the angled shadows of late afternoon and the soft diffusion of an overcast day add layers of mood and depth to a space. By embracing these qualities, you can create interiors that feel grounded, dynamic and alive.

← Afternoon light streams through sheer curtains in this Gold Coast penthouse. A floor-to-ceiling mirror amplifies the glow, reflecting both the space and the shifting light throughout the day.

LAYERING LIGHT: DEPTH AND DIMENSION

Layering your lighting can turn a flat, uninspiring space into one that feels dynamic, balanced and alive. Instead of relying on a single overhead fixture, think of light as having three levels: general, task and accent. Each layer contributes to the overall depth and character of the room, and when paired with thoughtful choices in tone and quality, the effect is transformative.

Overhead lighting provides the foundation, but should rarely stand alone. A dimmer can soften its intensity, while floor lamps and table lamps add warmth and create smaller pockets of illumination that make the space feel inviting. Accent lighting, such as wall sconces or LED strips, highlights architectural features or textured surfaces, casting subtle shadows that bring a sense of dimension and intrigue.

The temperature of the light also plays a role in the layering process. Warm lighting, with its golden tones, creates a cosy and intimate atmosphere, while cooler light is crisp and energising, ideal for areas where focus and clarity are essential. Combining these tones thoughtfully within a room enhances its versatility. For example, a seating area might benefit from warm table lamps that encourage relaxation, while cooler task lights nearby provide balance for more functional needs.

The quality of light, whether soft and diffused or sharp and focused, further shapes the mood and functionality of each layer. Diffused lighting, such as from frosted shades or fabric-covered lamps, wraps the room in a gentle glow, while focused beams highlight details and textures with precision.

LET'S TALK ABOUT THE 'BIG LIGHT'

We all know what the 'big light' is. The single overhead fixture that floods the entire room with brightness at the flick of a switch. It's functional, but it can be downright offensive to a well-designed space. The harsh, all-encompassing glare flattens textures, washes out colours and obliterates any sense of intimacy.

The big light has a function, but for everyday living, it is the lighting equivalent of shouting. A room feels much more inviting when the lighting is layered, with softer, smaller sources creating pools of warmth and focus.

↑ With three secondary light sources – the pendant, sconce and table lamp – this room offers flexibility in brightness and ambience. Each plays a role in shaping the mood, whether it's soft, directional or diffused.

HOW TO USE LIGHT TO SET A SCENE

Use brighter, cooler lights for functionality and sharper focus, but ensure they can be softened with dimmers or paired with warm accent lights for moments of relaxation or intimacy. The interplay of tones and qualities adds richness and flexibility, ensuring your lighting adapts to every occasion.

MOOD LIGHTING

Mood lighting is where design meets emotion. This is the layer of lighting that encourages relaxation and connection, transforming a space into a haven as the day winds down.

Rather than relying on a single source, mood lighting works best with multiple smaller lights. A table lamp on a sideboard can draw attention to a specific corner, while a softly glowing floor lamp near a sofa creates a cosy reading spot. Wall sconces or LED strips along shelving or architectural features bring depth and visual interest without overwhelming the room.

Candles and other ambient sources add a flickering warmth, elevating the mood. A cluster of candles on a dining table turns a simple meal into an occasion, while a single candle by the bed creates calm as you wind down.

HOW TO CREATE FOCUS WITH LAMPS

HIGHLIGHT KEY ZONES

Use lamps to draw attention to specific areas, like a reading chair, a console or a side table. This creates visual anchors and ensures every part of the room feels considered.

GUIDE THE EYE

Position lamps to create a sense of flow that leads the eye naturally through the space. For instance, a series of small table lamps can subtly define the edges of a larger room.

BALANCE SHADOWS

Lamps positioned at varying heights – on the floor, at table level and higher on shelves – will balance shadows and prevent the space from feeling too bright or flat.

TIPS AND TRICKS

01

TOO HARSH?

Replace cold bulbs with warmer ones, or use a diffuser to soften the glare.

02

NOT ENOUGH?

Add lamps at varying heights, like floor lamps and sconces, to fill the space.

03

FLAT?

Introduce accent lights to highlight features like artwork or architectural details.

04

OVERLY BRIGHT?

Use dimmers to adjust the intensity and create a more intimate ambience.

LET LIGHT LEAD THE WAY

Light is more than illumination. It is a storyteller that weaves emotion, function and beauty into the fabric of your home. It creates connection, defines atmosphere and reveals the intricate details that make a space uniquely yours. The interplay of natural and artificial light, when considered with care, breathes life into every corner, transforming an ordinary space into an extraordinary one.

Not just a simple utility, light is a quiet collaborator in your design. It invites warmth into your living spaces, heightens intimacy in quiet moments and energises areas where focus is needed. Thoughtful lighting doesn't just shape how your home looks, it shapes how it feels, guiding your experience of each room, every day.

Light is the unseen architect of your home, shaping spaces in ways that comfort, inspire and endure.

EDWARDS & Co Ltd

BETWEEN SHADOWS AND SUNLIGHT

In the heart of Surry Hills, where Sydney's creative pulse beats strongest, a lofty space stretches its arms wide to catch every fleeting ray of light. Housed within the bones of a 1920s warehouse, this apartment floats above the streets like a secret only the skyline knows, wedged gently between the shoulders of neighbouring buildings.

Cathedral-like windows invite the day in, in all its moods. Golden mornings spill across the century-old hardwood floors, while afternoons soften into silvered shadows that dance along the walls. This light is a character of its own, moving with grace and intention, filtering through the rippling forms of Akari lamps and casting gentle halos on the dining table.

Ellison Loft is both a canvas and a creation. The furniture whispers stories and every corner feels curated, yet lived in. A Wassily chair angles towards the window as if beckoning the sunlight, and a Huggy armchair waits patiently for the day to settle into evening. Layers of texture unfold in the quiet, plush upholstery, aged wood and smooth ceramics, all bathed in a light so generous it turns even the most mundane moments into art.

Outside, the alley hums with city life, but in this space, time stretches. This is a home that feels like it could belong to another city – perhaps a Tribeca loft, with its high ceilings and mood-lit nooks – but its soul is unmistakably Sydney. Here, the light holds memories, connection and the fleeting beauty of a moment bathed in its glow.

← The show-stopping Float sofa is drenched in the natural light that pours through the oversized warehouse windows. Hints of chrome and high gloss help to bounce the light around the space.

↑ A cosy corner to watch the city pass by the windows. The sculptural wall sconce adds a focused glow in the evening, while the large windows invite in ample daylight, balancing natural and artificial light throughout the day.

↓ The loft's floor-to-ceiling mirrors seem to double the size of the space. They make the room feel bigger and brighter, and also create a pretty great backdrop.

→ The oversized windows don't just bring in light, they help define the space. They act like a frame, subtly separating the lounge from the entry while keeping everything feeling open and connected.

↑ The amber glass? Totally intentional. It brings warmth to the neutral space and glows in the afternoon light, like a little golden-hour moment on the table.

→ The dining table that runs along the spine of the apartment is softly lit by Japanese paper pendants in different shapes. Their warm glow and placement balances the height of the space, and the sculptural wall light adds a subtle, artistic highlight.

→ At the opposite end of the apartment, the frosted warehouse windows let in plenty of light while keeping things private. The tree softens the space even more, casting dappled shadows over this little work spot.

↓ Every corner is an opportunity for a lamp – you can never have too many.

↑ The fluffy curved wall wraps around the bed, creating a cosy little retreat within the open space. As the sun goes down, the bedside pendants glow, making it feel even more cocooned.

↑ Natural light is controlled with block-out curtains for the bedroom spaces, a perfect balance of light and shadow when needed.

TWO

COLOUR

TWO

Colour, like spice, is a powerful tool. Some people go bold with cayenne and turmeric, others prefer a hint of cinnamon or a pinch of a subtle blend. The key is balance. Just as a great cook knows how to mix flavours to bring out the best in a dish, great interiors use colour to evoke emotion and enhance the character of a space.

'Life is about using the whole box of crayons.'

RUPAUL · 1960– · DRAG QUEEN AND TELEVISION HOST

The Bold Beginnings of Colour

When I was in high school, my parents gave me free rein to design my bedroom. It was my first taste of creative freedom and I threw myself into the project with unbridled enthusiasm. Armed with a paintbrush and a head full of ideas, I transformed my space into what I thought was the pinnacle of style. The result? A palette that could generously be called 'eclectic'. I chose three different shades of blue – two for the walls and one for the ceiling trim. I added a light brown feature wall for contrast and, for reasons I still can't quite explain, painted the ceiling a dark, red-toned brown.

Was it good? Not one bit. It was, in hindsight, a pretty rough palette, a mix of colours that didn't quite harmonise. But what I'm most grateful for is that my parents let me take that risk. They didn't question my choices or try to steer me towards something safer. They allowed me to experiment, to make mistakes and to see for myself the transformative power of colour. I still remember the thrill of standing in that room, paint drying on the walls, knowing that I had created something entirely my own.

That room sparked my passion for design. It also taught me an early lesson: colour has the power to shape a space, for better or worse. It showed me how colour could evoke emotions, alter perceptions and bring energy to a room. It was my first encounter with the magic and challenges of design.

Now, as a designer, I try to encourage people to embrace colour in their homes. It's not about perfection, it's about expression. Colour is a gateway to creativity, a way to bring personality and energy into a space. It's where decision-making begins, and where the magic often lies. When you decide to take a risk with colour, you are embracing the opportunity to create a home that feels uniquely yours.

Colour isn't just decorative; it speaks directly to our emotions and senses. It can shape mood, create atmosphere and make a space feel more personal. Colour often connects to personal emotions, which is why certain spaces may resonate more deeply for some people than others. A balanced palette can make a room feel cohesive, rather than chaotic, and contrasting colours can create depth and visual interest.

To harness the potential of colour, it is important to understand not just how colours look, but how they work together, how they affect our feelings and how to incorporate them thoughtfully into a home. By focusing on the key characteristics of colour, you can start to break down why a colour palette speaks to you and how it can translate into your own home. Observing colour in this way transforms it from a passive choice to an intentional design tool.

TONE SATURATION CONTRAST BALANCE EMOTION

KEY CHARACTERISTICS OF COLOUR

① TONE
Is it light or dark? Airy or moody? What kind of presence or emotional weight does it bring to the space?

② SATURATION
How intense or vivid is it? Is it soft and muted, or bold and vibrant?

③ CONTRAST
How do the colours work together? Do they clash in an exciting way or blend harmoniously?

④ BALANCE

Is one colour dominating the space, or is there a mix of hues?

⑤ EMOTION

How does the colour palette make you feel? Does it evoke calm, joy, nostalgia or excitement?

COLOUR FUNDAMENTALS

Let's start with the basics. The three primary colours – red, blue and yellow – are the foundation. The three secondary colours – green, orange and purple – are each created by mixing two primary colours. Complementary colours sit opposite each other on the colour wheel (for example, blue and orange) and offer dynamic contrast. Understanding these relationships helps to build a balanced, harmonious palette.

Every colour can be softened or deepened, creating tints, shades and tones. Playing with these variations adds dimension and depth to a palette.

BUILDING A COLOUR PALETTE

Building a colour palette is a process of discovery. The aim is to find a combination that feels both harmonious and uniquely yours. Experimentation is the key here. Give yourself permission to try, adjust and refine your palette until it feels right.

Begin with a colour that resonates with you. This could be a shade inspired by artwork, nature or a favourite object. Next, select a few complementary or analogous hues to add depth and harmony. A warm coral, for example, would pair beautifully with a soft teal or muted peach, creating a balanced base.

Layer your colours thoughtfully, testing them in context. Swatches of fabric, paint chips and decor items can help you see how they interact under different light conditions. If something feels off, don't hesitate to adjust your choices. Sometimes a slightly lighter shade or an additional neutral can bring a colour palette together.

Never dismiss neutral colours. They are essential for grounding a palette. Crisp whites, creams, greys and soft earthy tones provide a timeless foundation for any interior. They provide visual breathing room, allowing bolder hues to shine without overwhelming the space.

If you gravitate towards whites and prefer a more subtle palette, consider introducing tonal variations with natural colours like warm caramels, smoky charcoals or muted mushroom hues to add depth and character.

Neutral palettes can be just as dynamic as bolder schemes when layered thoughtfully. A room with white walls can come alive with textures in a neutral colour, such as a soft linen sofa, a natural sisal rug or timber accents.

Colour has the unique ability to transport us to specific locations or moments in time. Think of the sun-bleached hues of a Mediterranean village, the vibrant reds of an autumn forest, or the soft, muted tones of a foggy morning. These connections create deeply personal palettes, evoking memories of travels, seasons or cherished experiences.

A dusty rose might remind you of a favourite childhood jumper. A deep indigo could evoke a starry night on a family trip. By drawing from these inspirations, colour becomes more than decoration. It is a reflection of your story.

Colour is inherently tied to mood and memory. Each hue evokes an emotional response, creating an atmosphere that can transform a space.

Warm colours – reds, oranges and yellows – bring energy and intimacy. They are perfect for gathering spaces, like dining rooms or kitchens, where sociability thrives. Cool colours – blues, greens and purples – evoke calm and sophistication, making them ideal for bedrooms or spaces for quiet reflection. Neutrals – whites, greys and blacks – act as grounding elements. Depending on how they are used they can bring serenity or dramatic contrast to a space.

Whether you're seeking vibrancy or tranquillity, the emotional undertones of colour guide the way a room feels and how it invites people to interact.

TIPS AND TRICKS

01

TOO OVERWHELMING?

Soften it with neutrals or reduce the number of bold colours.

02

DISJOINTED COLOURS?

Introduce a bridging element, like a patterned rug or multicoloured artwork, to unify the space.

03

FEELING HESITANT?

Start small. Begin by adding colour through accents like cushions, throws or wall art before committing to larger surfaces.

Who says bathrooms have to be white? This rich green space, designed by Studio Esteta for Jumbled founder Pip Brett, proves that colour belongs everywhere. The moody walls change with the light, making the whole room feel calm and immersive.

COLOUR IN UNEXPECTED PLACES

Colour isn't just for walls. Adding it to unexpected areas can bring personality and surprise to your interiors. Ceilings, which are often overlooked, can become the 'fifth wall' of a space, where you can introduce soft pastels, bold hues or even metallic finishes. Painting a ceiling can alter the perception of height and draw the eye upward, adding an unexpected layer of interest.

Another creative use of colour is on trims, doorways and architectural details. Highlighting these features with contrasting or complementary hues creates a sense of rhythm and defines a space in subtle yet impactful ways. Painted furniture, such as sideboards or chairs, can turn them into statement pieces and infuse a room with vibrancy and individuality.

PLEASE, ENOUGH WITH THE FEATURE WALLS

We've all seen them – the lone wall bravely wearing a bold hue, surrounded by its plain siblings. It's meant to be a statement, but it often ends up looking like a wall that lost a bet. One lonely swathe of colour doesn't say, 'I love colour.' It says, 'I didn't have the nerve to commit.'

This is where colour drenching comes in. Instead of singling out one wall, why not go the other way entirely? Paint ALL the walls, the ceiling and even the trim in a single, saturated shade. This ultimate show of confidence creates a cohesive, enveloping environment that feels deliberate and bold.

The entire room gets to share the spotlight, and the result is a space that's striking, stylish and unquestionably intentional.

HOW TO TEST PAINT COLOURS

Sample pots are your best friend. Start with at least four options:

1. A colour you're immediately drawn to
2. A similar colour that is more or less saturated
3. A similar colour that is lighter or darker
4. A wild card – an unexpected colour that you love, but aren't sure will work.

Paint large swatches on your wall and observe them throughout the day. Light changes everything, and seeing colours in context helps you decide.

FASHIONS AND TRENDS

Trends can be a great starting point if you're feeling stuck or unsure about where to begin. They reflect the cultural and design zeitgeist, suggesting new ideas and palettes you may not have considered.

But trends are, by definition, temporary. Colours go in and out of fashion, so what feels fresh today may feel dated in a few years. That's why it is important to choose colours you genuinely love. Embrace colours that resonate with you, and remember that paint is never permanent. You can always redefine a space in the future.

↖ This tiny pop of red is a nod to the 'unexpected red theory' that flourished in 2024. It suggests that adding red in an unexpected place immediately elevates and enhances the look of a room.

↑ This deep blue bookshelf is a lesson in timeless design – rich, grounded, and built to last. The red accents add just enough contrast to keep it feeling fresh, but the overall palette will not date.

Have you heard that dark paint makes a room feel smaller? Total myth. Deep tones can create a sense of depth and cosiness, making the space feel rich, layered and inviting.

Colour is both deeply personal and endlessly versatile. It carries the power to evoke emotion, tell a story, and transform a house into a home. Whether you embrace bold, saturated hues or prefer the serenity of neutrals, the key is to let colour reflect who you are and how you want to feel in your space. Trust your instincts, take risks, and remember: every colour choice is a step closer to creating a home that feels uniquely yours.

A PALETTE OF POSSIBILITY

IN THE GOLDEN HEART of Coopers Shoot, where rolling hills meet endless sky, Sun Ranch unfurls like a dream painted in vibrant strokes. This is not merely a dwelling, it is a living canvas. Colour dances with texture and the land whispers its stories into every corner.

This home is a celebration of contrasts, blending the sunlit ease of Californian ranch houses with the dusty allure of Spaghetti Westerns and the playful boldness of Australian design. The palette is drawn directly from the surrounding landscape – ochres and rusts echo the soils, deep greens capture the hills, and cerulean and saffron burst into view like wildflowers after rain. Inside and out, the hues seem to shift with the light, creating a space as dynamic as the land it inhabits.

Every detail tells a story. Painted patterns on the walls create striking bedheads, their intricate designs adding a handcrafted elegance that feels both timeless and unexpected. The surprisingly bold contrasts of the doorframes transform thresholds into moments of delight. In the living spaces, vintage leather chairs and bespoke furnishings sit alongside sun-drenched textiles and ceramics that shimmer like found treasures. Communal spaces like the Whiskey Lounge and the Long House Kitchen invite you to linger, their warm tones embracing the rhythms of the day. Outside, the gardens bloom with life, horses graze lazily in the distance and the horizon stretches endlessly, as if inviting you to dream.

As the day draws to a close, the ranch transforms. Shadows lengthen, and the setting sun ignites the sky in waves of deep pinks and purples. This is a moment to pause by the fire, a glass in hand, and watch the day melt into evening. At Sun Ranch, colour is more than an aesthetic. It is a way of being, a reminder that the best designs are those that challenge you to live boldly and linger long.

↖ **PREVIOUS** Welcome to Sun Ranch, a hideaway that blends 1970s California nostalgia with global influences. Vintage furniture, a warm, bold palette and playful patterns invite you to kick off your cowboy boots and settle into a space that feels both adventurous and effortlessly relaxed.

← The Lair is a sunken lounge that is designed for gatherings and quiet moments around the sculptural fireplace. The room is wrapped in terracotta tiles, from floor to column. The colour isn't just a backdrop – it sets the tone, creating a space that feels warm and vibrant.

↓ Dedar's 'Tiger Mountain' velvet fabric brings a golden glow to The Lair, playing off the terracotta tiles like a Byron Bay sunrise.

↑ The tiger motif also sneaks into the private suites, this time against olive-green walls. The deeper tones add another layer, setting these rooms apart from the earthy warmth of the Long House.

← Golden light and olive walls create a warm, layered space – perfect for slowing down and soaking in the surroundings.

↑ The contrast of peach motifs on olive walls brings a folk-art feel, and handpainted details add a personal touch and a crafted element.

← The contrasting khaki tiles and green concrete create a striking backdrop in this bathroom, where natural light and plants bring vibrancy and life, softening the strong colour palette.

→ ↓ The warm browns of the timber set the stage for some serious ranch charm – cowboy portraits, straw hats, and a little giddy-up to keep things lively.

←← Rich timber walls frame these vibrant bathrooms, where the warm, sunset-inspired palette of reds, pinks and yellows evokes the soft glow of dusk.

← The checkerboard tiles cut through the horizon of the bathroom, acting like a sweeping sunset and an unexpected flair of colour.

↓ No bedhead? No worries. In these deep terracotta-painted rooms, bedheads are painted directly onto the walls, and accented with pops of cobalt and magenta for a bold, artistic touch.

↑ Colour blocking can help a space feel defined and create a hierarchy between zones. Here, the intense cobalt blue walls almost fade into the background, allowing the bold yellow, magenta and orange tiles to take centre stage.

→ By keeping the design ideas consistent, but playing with a shared palette, each room develops its own personality.

← Look up! The ceiling in this tiny powder room is a real highlight. The concentric stripes pull focus in all the best ways.

↓ Again, complementary tones sing in this space. Deep blues with warm terracotta make for a perfect match.

← Never forget about colour theory – even classic colour combos can feel bold and exciting. Blue and orange are complementary colours, and a big dose of both makes for a bathroom like no other.

← Unexpected pops of colour in more ways than one. Deep red walls? A cobalt blue doorframe? And yet, somehow, this corner of the Long House feels soothing and quiet.

↑ Playing on the global influences, collected objects add hints of colour and casual rustic charm to the raw timber shelves.

Whiskey business! The deep reds of the Whiskey Lounge invite you to kick up your boots and take a load off. Stevie Nicks croons softly from the record player as you sip your drinks and welcome the evening. The perfect ending to a day at Sun Ranch.

THREE

PATTERN

THREE

Pattern is like a signature flavour woven through a meal – the lemon zest brightening every course, or the spice that lingers after each bite. It creates rhythm, tying a space together. Bold patterns are like a hit of chilli or a burst of fresh herbs – vibrant and full of personality. Subtle patterns add depth without overpowering. The key, as in cooking, is knowing when to repeat and when to hold back.

'No pattern should be without some sort of meaning.'

WILLIAM MORRIS · 1834-1896 · TEXTILE DESIGNER

A Love Affair with Pattern

When I started working as a style editor for magazines, I didn't realise how much it would shape my approach to design. Unlike working with clients, where every decision is tailored to someone else's needs, I had creative freedom. This role was about sparking ideas and inspiring readers, not adhering to strict briefs. I could push boundaries, take risks and experiment in ways I'd never done before.

I fell in love with pattern gradually, over years of photo shoots, set designs and editorial spreads. Each issue was a new opportunity to test unexpected pairings, combining graphic rugs with ornate wallpapers, layering prints over textures and finding harmony in what initially seemed chaotic. Some combinations were triumphs, others were lessons learned. But every risk taught me more about the power of pattern to shape mood, tell a story and bring a unique rhythm to a space.

That philosophy came to life in one of my favourite projects, a house that I worked on with my husband, Ryan. The brief was 'Italian summer meets Australian coast', and the clients gave us the freedom to experiment. From playful tiles to painterly wallpapers, every surface became an opportunity to tell a story. It was a joyful exploration of pattern that felt fresh, yet deeply rooted in the personalities of the space and its owners.

Pattern is much more than just decoration. It is a tool for storytelling, and a way to bring energy, depth and personality into a home. But it's also about the art of restraint – knowing when to stop and when to let a bold choice speak for itself. That is the magic of pattern. Daring yet disciplined, playful yet purposeful.

Repetition, shape and movement bring life and personality to a space. Bold patterns are energising, and subtle ones are soothing. Learning to observe and analyse the key characteristics of pattern can help you understand why some designs work well in a room and resonate with you. When you can identify and understand these characteristics, you will start to see how pattern can shape a room's personality, guide the eye and create a rhythm that brings a space alive.

FOCUS SCALE LAYERING PLACEMENT INTERACTION

KEY CHARACTERISTICS OF PATTERN

① FOCUS

What is the main patterned element in the space? Is it a bold rug, the wallpaper or the upholstery? What is the visual hierarchy?

② SCALE

Is the pattern large and graphic or small and intricate? How does its scale affect the mood of the space?

③ LAYERING

How are they combined? Are they layered with solids, textures or other patterns? Do they share colours or themes that tie them together?

④ PLACEMENT

Are they on floors, walls, furniture or accessories? Do they dominate the space, or do they feel subtle?

⑤ INTERACTION

How do they interact with the colours, textures and light in the room? Do they blend harmoniously or create a deliberate contrast?

TYPES OF PATTERNS

Patterns come in countless forms, each evoking a different mood and style. Understanding the different types of patterns will help you decide which ones align with your vision.

TRADITIONAL

Plaid, checks and stripes are classic patterns that offer warmth and familiarity. Their regular repetition brings a timeless quality to a design.

GEOMETRIC

Defined by shapes and repetition, geometric patterns create structure and rhythm, adding a fun, modern feel to a print.

ABSTRACT

Abstract patterns are less defined and more interpretive, often adding a sense of movement and creativity to a space.

CULTURAL

The cultural roots of patterns like paisley, damask and ikat bring history and storytelling to a textile.

FLORAL

From delicate blossoms to bold botanical prints, floral patterns add a natural, romantic touch to interiors.

ORGANIC

Organic patterns often mimic waves, clouds or foliage and create a soothing, grounded atmosphere.

→ Don't be afraid to mix patterns of different shapes, sizes and textures. This teen room is bold in theory but the cohesive tones keep it feeling quiet despite the contrasting patterns of the wallpaper and fabrics.

WHAT GOES AROUND COMES AROUND

Every few years, a certain pattern is declared dated. Remember when chevron was everywhere? Floors, pillows, coffee mugs… it became so overdone that it was practically banned from design conversations. But fashion trends are like old friends – they show up again when you least expect it. One day you're rolling your eyes at leopard print, the next you're layering it on a throw and feeling just the right amount of rebellious.

Patterns are cyclical. What feels passé today might feel nostalgic and fresh tomorrow. So, don't be too quick to judge a pattern as over. It's all about how you use it. A touch of something that has fallen out of favour can feel daring and clever and completely new.

PATTERN IN MATERIALITY

Pattern in materiality transforms surfaces into tactile, and visually engaging elements, adding depth and character to a space.

TILES AND WALLPAPER

Tiles and wallpaper are two of the easiest ways to incorporate pattern into a space. Tiles are a durable and functional medium that can be used on floors, splashbacks or walls. Classic layouts like herringbone or checkerboard feel timeless, while bold designs can make a statement. Wallpaper can transform a blank wall into a canvas for creativity through large-scale murals, intricate repeats or subtle tone-on-tone designs. Both materials add a tactile quality to pattern, elevating it from mere visual interest to a design element you can touch and interact with.

PAINT

Paint is a versatile and accessible way to introduce pattern into your home. It allows for creative expression, from framing doorways with contrasting trims to painting bedheads in bold shapes. Folk art–inspired motifs on furniture can add a playful, handcrafted feel.

Unlike more permanent materials, paint offers the freedom to experiment and change your mind. If it doesn't work, you can always paint over it. This flexibility makes paint an excellent medium for trying out patterns without making a long-term commitment.

NATURAL MATERIALS

Not all patterns are the product of a design process. Nature offers its own stunning motifs through materials like stone and timber. These natural patterns can add depth, authenticity and a sense of calm or drama to interiors.

STONE VEINING

Marble and quartz slabs feature unique, unrepeatable veins that feel organic and luxurious.

WOOD GRAINS

Timber species such as oak, walnut and even burl offer distinct grain patterns, from smooth and linear to knotty and complex.

SHELL INLAYS

Natural shells create iridescent patterns that bring a touch of the ocean indoors.

HOW TO WORK WITH NATURAL PATTERNS

PLACEMENT MATTERS

Use natural patterns in areas where they can be appreciated up close, like countertops or furniture surfaces.

VARIATION IS KEY

Embrace the imperfections and irregularities of natural materials; they add character and uniqueness.

LIGHTING EFFECTS

Consider how light interacts with the material, highlighting its depth and detail.

BALANCE WITH SOLIDS

Pair natural patterns with solid colours or subtle textures to avoid visual overload.

LONGEVITY

Natural patterns often have timeless appeal, making them a worthwhile investment for enduring beauty.

↑ Coastal calm is the vibe of this apartment. A hint of wallpaper is paired with a patterned chair and layers of neutral-on-neutral decor.

NEUTRAL-ON-NEUTRAL PATTERN

Patterns don't always have to be bold and eye-catching. Subtle, tone-on-tone patterns can add just as much depth and interest to a space. A soft stripe in neutral colours will bring a quiet elegance to walls or textiles without dominating the room. A fine check or a delicate floral can blend into the background while still adding texture and complexity. These understated patterns work beautifully in layered designs, creating a harmonious, cohesive look that is rich in detail without being overwhelming.

The scale of a pattern also plays a crucial role. A small-scale print on a sofa or chair may look like a solid colour from a distance, but its intricacy is revealed on closer inspection. This approach is perfect for adding subtle interest to a space, proving that pattern doesn't have to shout to be effective.

TIPS AND TRICKS

01

START SMALL

If you're unsure, begin with patterned cushions or throws before committing to larger elements like wallpaper or rugs.

02

LIMIT YOUR PALETTE

Stick to a cohesive colour scheme to ensure the patterns are working together, rather than competing.

03

USE NEGATIVE SPACE

Give patterns room to breathe by balancing them with solid colours or textures.

04

EXPERIMENT WITH PLACEMENT

Try patterns in unexpected places. Wallpaper a ceiling or tile staircase risers.

05

BALANCE BOLDNESS

Pair a statement pattern with more subdued elements to keep the design grounded.

06

TOO BUSY?

Remove one patterned element and reassess. Often, less is more.

07

TOO SAFE?

Add a single bold pattern to inject personality and energy into the space.

Pattern offers a rhythmic backdrop to daily life. It can be a subtle, or sometimes bold, refrain that can tie a room together – or unravel it if misapplied. Like adding harmonies to a melody, patterns can support, contrast or highlight other design elements. Done well, they add movement and identity, allowing the space to breathe and evolve. Whether you favour intricate tapestries or gentle, tone-on-tone illusions, remember that patterns, like verses of a poem, should have room to echo and resonate. In that balance of repetition and negative space is a visual cadence that is both artful and dynamic.

THE MEDITERRANEAN MUSE

On Sydney's Northern Beaches, a 1970s house has been transformed into a love letter to pattern, where Italian influences dance with the ebb and flow of family life. Patterns are not used as decoration, they are a language, weaving stories into the fabric of this home. Each room is a chapter, its textures and motifs telling a tale of transformation and connection.

Upstairs, simplicity sets the stage for the ocean's grandeur. White walls frame sweeping views of deep navy waters, and these calm expanses are mirrored in the home's palette. The kitchen features patterned tiles reminiscent of Mediterranean courtyards under the Portofino sun. The over-the-top charm of their handpainted designs ground the space without pulling focus. The fireplace, adorned with zellige tiles and navy basket-weave wallpaper, adds a tactile rhythm to the room, its layers inviting warmth and curiosity.

Downstairs, the patterns become more personal and expressive. The master bedroom feels like a private suite in a luxurious hideaway. The hand-illustrated wallpaper depicts soft, abstract botanicals that weave a narrative of coastal dunes and imagined gardens. The child's room blooms with playful pinks, the wardrobe adorned with delicate handpainted details, while the family bathroom feels alive with aqua-and-white tiles accented by pink trims and individually painted tiled counters. It is a celebration of craft and joy. Even the laundry delights, with gingham floors and a green shibori blind adding a cheerful flourish.

This is a house where patterns whisper stories and invite connection. It presents a vibrant mosaic of family life framed by the romance of the Mediterranean and the calm of the Australian coast.

← The main living room of Newport House was inspired by the ever-changing blue tones of the ocean. The basket-weave wallpaper acts as a patterned base to build upon, with each element subtly adding its own tactile pattern and materiality.

↑ The sunken lounge invites you to curl up and watch the weather roll by. Natural organic patterns in the coffee table complement the more geometric shapes in the ombre rug, which in turn are reflected in the painterly fabric designs of the cushions.

↑ Zellige tiles are handcrafted Moroccan clay tiles known for their vibrant colours, rustic hand-cut edges and glossy finish. Here, they are used as a splashback, and their irregularities create a colour pattern play.

↑ An Italian-inspired tile sits above the striking yellow cooktop and oven. This bold tile is used sparingly in the kitchen, evoking a moment in the sun on an Italian coast,

Where the living room sinks into deeper blues, the kitchen keeps things light, closer to the surface. There's pattern in the materiality of the tiles and the natural grains of wood and marble. It's all about balance and restraint – no individual material pulls focus.

← ↑ The main ensuite throws all the rules out, mixing stripes with checks and featuring a multicoloured marble floor. And yet, there's a calm to it. The neutral palette is quiet, and a hint of ocean blue dots the horizon in a trim tile.

↑ The hardworking laundry space is not forgotten. Simple tile arrangements create a gingham floor of greens and neutrals.

→ Cultures and patterns clash, but sticking to the palette ties it all together. The blind hints at shibori – a traditional Japanese dyeing technique that involves folding, twisting or binding fabric to create unique patterned designs.

← Handpainted joinery adds a geometric flair to this pink paradise. The traditional gingham of the carpet is echoed on the fronts of the wardrobe doors, layering patterns and styles seamlessly.

↑ Dusty sprigs decorate the soft pink walls, almost becoming a solid backdrop that allows the rest of the room to shine. There are patterns, striped curtains, floral wallpaper, gingham cupboards and ikat cushions, but nothing feels out of place.

← The family bathroom brings tones of blue and red, evoking sorbet by the sand. A thin-striped red-and-white roman blind frames the window above the bath, adding a touch of flair and whimsy to this busy hub.

↑ The hero of this space is the tiled countertop. These handpainted tiles bring the European summer story to the forefront, with the undulating blue-toned tiles lapping like soft waves in the background, and framed by a strong red trim tile.

↑ → The main suite is surrounded by painterly wallpaper that is reminiscent of soft sand dunes, bringing the patterns to a hush. Soft blue curtains blend into the view beyond the windows, and a hint of geometry in the bed cover adds just enough strong design to this retreat.

FOUR

TEXTURE

FOUR

Texture is like the layering of ingredients that makes a meal interesting. Think of a great pasta dish: silky sauce, al dente pasta, a crunch of toasted breadcrumbs – it's all about contrast. In interiors, combining soft and hard, or smooth and rough, adds that same irresistible depth.

‘The use of texture in design is not just about how things feel, it’s about how they look too.’

KELLY HOPPEN · 1959– · INTERIOR DESIGNER

The Tactile Heartbeat of Design

When my sister asked me to help design her apartment, I was excited, but also a little unsure. She loves minimalism and neutrals, while I gravitate towards bold colours and vibrant patterns. I wasn't sure how I could create a space that would feel uniquely hers, without defaulting to my usual style. The original space had been pared back to its essentials – white walls and pale wood floors. It felt calm, but lacked the warmth and personality I strive for in my projects.

I turned to texture. I realised that if we weren't going to layer in colour or pattern, we could build depth through touch and tone. We started with a very inviting, soft, nubby linen sofa in a muted shade. Next came a thick wool rug that added both warmth and a tactile, grounding presence. An organic stone coffee table had a rough surface that was full of natural variation. We lime-washed the walls, giving them a subtle texture and depth without pulling focus. A collection of handmade ceramics – some matte, some glossy, all uniquely imperfect – added subtle layers of interest. Vintage timber chairs, with organic forms and worn surfaces, introduced a rich, storied element.

As the space evolved, I saw how powerful texture can be in a minimalist setting. Without loud colours or prints, the apartment took on a quiet sophistication. Each layer of texture brought a new dimension, making the room feel thoughtful and intentional, yet still calm and restrained. Just as my sister wanted. Designing her apartment taught me that texture is more than a supporting act, it is a star in its own right.

Cabbage Tree House in Bayview redefines the limits of textures in a space. It seamlessly blends indoor and outdoor spaces through connective brickwork, and the cooler textures, such as concrete, are softened with woven rugs and natural timbers.

Textures are more than just how a material feels on your skin, they can bring character and depth to a room. They define the depth and visual impact of a space and can make it feel dynamic and engaging, adding richness without being overwhelming.

Observing texture will help you understand how it interacts with light, materials and space to tell a cohesive design story. When you focus on these key characteristics, texture becomes more than a background detail. It will be a tool you can use to give a space soul and make it come alive.

CONTRAST DEFINITION MATERIAL PLACEMENT INTEGRATION

KEY CHARACTERISTICS OF TEXTURE

① CONTRAST

How do the textures play off each other?

② DEFINITION

How pronounced is the texture? Is it bold, like exposed brick or raw timber, or subtle, like a smooth plaster wall or soft velvet cushion?

③ MATERIAL

What materials dominate the space? What are their tactile qualities? Are they warm and inviting, like wood and stone, or cool and modern, like metal and glass?

④ PLACEMENT

Where is texture used in the room? On large surfaces like walls and floors, or smaller accents like furniture and decor?

⑥ INTEGRATION

Do the textures feel cohesive? Do they complement each other or do they clash?

My family's farmhouse is a haven, an escape, and holds our history. It is a study in warmth and texture – every surface, from the stone fireplace to the soft furnishings, invites you to settle in and relax.

UNDERSTANDING MATERIALITY

Texture carries emotional and functional weight. It speaks of comfort, luxury, history and nature, while adding depth and variety to a space. From the warmth of a handwoven rug to the sleek coolness of polished stone, texture creates a sensory connection to your home that can't be ignored.

At the heart of texture is materiality – the inherent qualities of the materials you choose and how they look, feel and interact with their environment. Every surface in a room, from a rugged stone wall to a smooth leather chair, contributes to the overall atmosphere. The visible grain of a weathered oak table conveys character and a rich history, while a sleek glass tabletop adds lightness and refinement.

Understanding the materiality of these elements allows you to select textures that not only feel good but create a cohesive and balanced design.

PHYSICAL VS VISUAL TEXTURE

PHYSICAL TEXTURE

This is what you feel with your fingertips. The grain of raw wood, the nubbiness of a boucle chair, the cool irregularity of natural stone. These tangible textures invite touch and add warmth, character or luxury to a space. Whether through joinery, wall textures or furniture, physical texture creates a sensory experience that connects us to the environment around us.

VISUAL TEXTURE

Think of the subtle illusions created by a printed fabric, a trompe l'oeil wallpaper or a glossy ceramic tile. Even without a tactile element, visual textures can add richness and depth. A patterned rug, for instance, can create the impression of texture and movement, even if it feels smooth underfoot. Combining physical and visual textures thoughtfully results in a layered, multidimensional look.

BUILDING TEXTURE FROM THE GROUND UP

Just as a recipe often starts with a base, broth, dough or batter, texture begins with the largest surfaces – floors, walls and ceilings.

FLOORING

Polished hardwood or rugged slate can anchor a room with natural warmth or cool solidity. Each plank or slab tells its own story through knots, veins and subtle variations. And, even in a room with hard floors, rugs add immediate softness. A high-pile rug can turn an austere space into a cosy retreat, while a flat weave or sisal mat introduces gentle earthiness.

WALLS AND CEILINGS

When choosing paint, consider not only the colour, but the finish. A matte surface absorbs light for a quiet elegance, but a satin or semi-gloss finish bounces light, emphasising colour and vibrancy.

And remember that walls don't have to be smooth and plain. Textured paints like limewash, microcement, or French wash can add subtle dimension, while maintaining a soft, organic feel. They add both visual and physical texture to a room, enhancing the interplay of light and shadow on a surface.

Grass cloth or fabric-backed wallpaper brings a subtle texture to a space, like a gentle hum in the background. Wood panelling, exposed brick and decorative mouldings make a dramatic statement.

Consider leaving some materials exposed. Brick and stone walls bring raw, authentic texture to unexpected places, and can define a focal point that grounds a space in natural elements.

MAJOR FURNITURE

Linen, velvet and leather upholstery each set a distinct tone. Velvet hints at luxury, linen whispers of breezy afternoons, and leather ages gracefully, telling tales of everyday use.

Textures need contrast to bring balance to a space. Concrete with rattan, brick with glass, the different textures of indoors and outdoors. Bring them all together to create something truly unique.

LAYERING TEXTURES FOR DEPTH

Once the foundational surfaces of an interior are in place, layers of texture add richness and personality, bringing harmony and depth to the design. Combining smooth and rough elements, like polished stone with rustic wood or sleek metal with woven materials, adds interest and balance to an interior. Upholstery choices – boucle, velvet, linen, leather – contribute character to a space and influence whether it feels luxurious, breezy or grounded. Throws and cushions introduce softness and variety, while decorative accents like ceramics, glass and metal provide visual contrast and tactile interest. The interplay between these elements – soft against hard, matte against sleek – creates a dynamic, multidimensional room that invites touch and exploration.

Piling on different textiles without cohesion can make a space feel unsettled.

CARPET DIEM (BUT NOT EVERYWHERE)

Once upon a time, carpet ruled the world. Floors? Carpet. Stairs? Carpet. Bathrooms? Carpet. Even the toilet lid got its own fuzzy little crown. No surface was safe from the clutches of synthetic pile.

And, sure, it was cosy. Until it wasn't. Let's be honest – what feels snug in the bedroom gets downright weird in the bathroom. The problem wasn't carpet itself, it was carpet in places it clearly didn't belong.

That is the real lesson here. Texture can transform a room, if it's in the right space. A thick rug underfoot in the living room? Fantastic. But move that same plushness into the bathroom, and you've wandered into uncomfortable territory.

Before you commit to a texture, consider its surroundings. The right texture in the right space doesn't just look good, it feels right.

TIPS AND TRICKS

01

TOO CROWDED?

Focus on a few key textures – perhaps a woven upholstered chair paired with a smooth oak table – and let those elements shine. Too much variety can distract rather than delight.

02

TOO BUSY?

Use your negative space. Let textures breathe by balancing them with simpler surfaces. A rough stone fireplace will stand out more dramatically against smooth plaster walls.

03

TOO FLAT?

Add a bold textural accent – a woven tapestry on the wall, a chunky braided rug or a sculptural lamp. Focus on one statement piece rather than scattering lots of small items.

04

OVERWHELMING?

Pare it down to a few main textures. Keep large surfaces like floors and walls understated. Let one or two items – a velvet armchair or a stone fireplace – do the talking.

Texture breathes empathy into design, affecting our senses in ways colour and form can't always reach. By blending smooth and rugged, shiny and matte, soft and sturdy, you can create a tapestry of sensation that resonates on a deeply human level. Just as a masterful chef combines creamy and crunchy elements to make a balanced dish, a skilled designer orchestrates textures so that each corner of a room invites exploration. In the gentle friction between surfaces, we find warmth, memory and a sense of home. This tactile heartbeat makes a space feel alive.

ROBERT STILIN
FRIDAYS FROM THE GARDEN
GILLES & BOISSIER

A SYMPHONY OF SURFACES

From the outside, Sonoma Barn sits quietly, a humble silhouette in a golden sprawl of olive groves and vineyards. But when you step through its doors, the world shifts. What was once a simple, rectangular structure is now an ode to texture and transformation. Every surface speaks in whispers of craft and care.

Texture defines this home. Walls coated in velvety plaster soften the light, their subtle undulations speaking to a process of both technique and artistry. Arches carved from clay and cane rise unexpectedly, breaking the barn's original linearity and inviting movement. Your eye, your hand and your body are drawn forward. Even the ceilings have been carefully considered; their engineered trusses and layered finishes add depth and drama.

In the living spaces, softness abounds. Mohair curtains spill to the floor, their mossy green hue grounding the room, while lush upholstery invites touch and comfort. The kitchen is a study in contrast. Smooth quartzite counters meet the hand-carved, three-dimensional grain of ebony-stained wood – the wall feels more like sculpture than surface.

Each piece in this house feels intentional: a coffee table with raw, organic curves anchors one corner, while a bench, shaped as much by intuition as by tools, holds space in another. The dining table, which is so heavy it had to be craned into place, is a monument to the craftsmanship that defines this home.

Sonoma Barn is not just a house; it is a map drawn in texture, a journey where every surface tells a story and every detail reveals something new. Here, beauty lies not in perfection but in the depth and complexity of materials that feel as alive as the landscape outside.

↑ **PREVIOUS** This interior is a banquet of textures that mixes life, work and play. Every surface is adorned in materiality that comes alive when combined.

What started as a blank canvas has been transformed into a world of texture. Large rendered arches frame rooms that are treasure troves of contrast and materials.

← ↑ Downstairs, the office takes shape with Marmorino plaster walls and travertine floors in a French lay pattern. The grand curved staircase wraps up the space leading to the living zones, linking the two areas through materiality.

← ↓ The designers added architectural form and detail to what was essentially an empty box. Classic materiality and shape gives history and story to this new structure.

←↑ Texture is connected through shape and form in this living space. Soft curves from the seating link to the arches in the sideboard, and even the harder stones and marbles have rounded shapes to bring the visual language together.

↓ ↘ Colour brings texture and materiality together in these smaller spaces. The layered fluting of the green curtains is echoed in the legs of a table and the colours of the marbling in the vanity are picked up in the plaster walls and zellige floors.

← ↑ The forms of this kitchen mimic the arches seen throughout the home. The visual textures of the kitchen stone sit next to the physical textures of the floors and walls, all set in dramatic archways and curves.

← ↑ The textured walls guide you from one space to the next, and lead you into the bedroom with its soft, calming tones.

↙ ↓ A cascade of deep chocolate zellige tiles envelop this kitchenette, challenging typical applications of this material. The rolling curves and deep tones are mirrored in the vintage furniture and handcrafted pieces that decorate the spaces.

↑ Sonoma Barn is so unassuming from the outside that no-one would guess at the wonders that lie within, but the colours taken from the surrounding landscape hint at what can be found inside.

FIVE

LAYERS

FIVE

A great dish never hits just one note. It's built in layers, from base flavours to finishing touches. Interiors are no different. Every home has foundational elements, but it's the layering of furniture, textiles and decor that makes a space feel rich and full of life.

'A room should feel collected, not decorated. It's collecting and layering to create a style entirely one's own.'

ROMAN ALONSO · 1966– · INTERIOR DESIGNER

Layers of Life

For years, when I was asked to describe my personal style, I called myself a 'curated maximalist'. I was drawn to bold, collected interiors full of character and personality. But over time, I realised that label didn't quite fit. Some of my favourite spaces are minimalist, yet warm and full of life. Others are richly layered, telling stories in compelling detail.

The common element of these spaces wasn't maximalism or minimalism, it was layering. Layering brings depth, dimension and personality to a room. It's the magic trick that turns a blank canvas into something that feels alive, inviting and complete. It's not about adding everything at once, it's about curating with care and intention.

My own home is layered with objects that carry memories and meaning while creating a visual filter through the space. Each layer adds texture and nuance, making the rooms feel personal and dynamic. My balcony is a jungle oasis that seamlessly connects indoors and outdoors. The plants create a layered effect, softening the edges of the space while filtering light and adding depth, enhancing the interior's textures and colours.

Layering isn't about abundance; it's about balance. It is about understanding contrast, texture and proportion, and how they work together to elevate a space. Layers give a room warmth, character and quiet magic. They turn a house into a home that feels intentional, personal and alive.

My apartment, my home, my sanctuary. This space helped me shape how I function as a designer. Curated, colourful and layered with years of design decisions and experiments.

Layering is the relationship between elements in a room and how they interact to create depth, balance and flow. It's not about piling on more but about achieving harmony through thoughtful combinations.

PROPORTION MATERIALITY CONTRAST DEPTH CONNECTION

KEY CHARACTERISTICS OF LAYERS

① **PROPORTION**

Are the layers balanced? Do foundational pieces, like furniture, support smaller accents without competing?

② **MATERIALITY**

Are the materials fighting each other to dominate the space, or are they working together?

③ **CONTRAST**

How do forms and shapes interact? Could organic curves soften the sharp edges of linear designs?

④ DEPTH

Are the layers guiding the eye? Do they create dimension, drawing you into the space?

⑤ CONNECTION

How do the layers tie the room together? Do repeated colours, materials or shapes create cohesion?

PROPORTION ANCHORS A LAYERED SPACE

Proportion is the quiet hero of layering. It creates a balance between the bold and the subtle, ensuring that no element feels out of place. Foundational pieces, like sofas, dining tables and beds, provide structure so that smaller accents can shine.

To anchor a space, start with the largest items. A substantial sofa or table will set the tone, while smaller elements, like lamps, side tables or decor, add nuance. Think of the way that a delicate vase complements the weight of a timber table, or how a soft throw draped over a structured armchair creates subtle contrast.

Height and scale are equally important. Layering objects at varying heights keeps the eye moving and the space dynamic. A bold rug can define a room, and a smaller one layered on top can create focus without being overwhelming.

Proportion is about relationships. Bold pieces may draw attention first, but it's the smaller, quieter layers that complete the harmony. By balancing size, placement and height, you can create a room that feels considered, intentional and easy to inhabit.

STOP THE CHOP!

Ah, the cushion chop! That dramatic crease that is meant to scream 'I've been styled!' But does it really? It can make cushions look stiff and uninviting – more like props than pieces meant to be enjoyed.

Cushions should feel approachable. A casually arranged mix of different sizes, textures and shapes creates a relaxed, lived-in vibe.

So let's skip the theatrics. Let them sprawl naturally – it's part of their charm.

MATERIALITY ADDS PERSONALITY

Materials are the building blocks of a layered interior. Timber adds warmth, stone provides grounding, glass offers lightness, and textiles introduce softness and comfort. The thoughtful combination of these materials creates a rich and dynamic space.

Glass is an especially versatile material. Fluted or dimpled glass obscures a view and diffuses light while creating movement and subtle texture. Coloured or stained glass can filter sunlight, casting delicate hues across a room. Framed glass walls or steel partitions create visual boundaries without closing off spaces, offering both connection and division.

Textiles play a vital role in layering. They can add softness, enhance privacy and play with light, enriching the layers of a space. Sheer curtains that filter daylight create a gentle glow and provide privacy. Heavier drapes or woven blinds ground a room, control the light and insulate the space. Rugs can be used to define zones and add tactile depth, while cushions and throws provide colour, texture and a sense of ease. Combining different fabrics enhances the visual and tactile appeal of a room, making it feel dynamic yet cohesive.

Materiality is about creating balance through contrast. Repeating materials, like the brass of a door knob being echoed in a light fixture, adds subtle cohesion. When layered thoughtfully, materials bring depth, light and personality to your design.

↑ → This family kitchen in Bondi, designed by Studio Pulp, makes the most of a small space with clever planning. The colours, patterns, materials and shapes are layered on top of each other to maximise the footprint while keeping it personal and unique.

JULIUS ROBERTS
Ellie's Table
Toddler to Table

HOW TO ADD DEPTH USING LAYERS

Thoughtfully placed layers create depth that feels effortless. A curtain swaying in the breeze, a plush rug over hardwood floors or the interplay of a leafy plant against light creates a room that feels dynamic and alive.

ANCHOR CORNERS

Use tall plants, bold furniture or standing lamps to provide visual weight and create focus.

OVERLAP ELEMENTS

Combine rugs, curtains and furnishings to guide the eye through the room.

FRAME VIEWS

Position greenery or decor to create sight lines, drawing attention deeper into the space.

DEPTH: GUIDING THE EYE THROUGH LAYERS

Greenery has become a staple for bringing life into interiors, but the indoor jungle trend often leaned on excess. Instead of crowding a space, consider how plants can be layered thoughtfully to create depth and connection.

A tall plant, like a fiddle leaf fig, can anchor a corner, adding height and grounding the room. Smaller plants on shelves or sideboards guide the eye through the space, and hanging or trailing varieties soften edges and add flow.

Placing plants near windows or doorways to frame a balcony or garden view blurs the boundary between indoors and outdoors. Matching planters inside and out enhances this connection.

Thoughtful layering of greenery softens spaces, introduces organic shapes and creates a natural, cohesive interior without overwhelming it.

HOW TO USE FORM AND SHAPE

BREAK UP LINES

Use organic shapes, like a free-form rug or a sculptural vase, to soften the rigid lines of architectural features or structured furniture.

ADD VISUAL INTEREST

Incorporate overlapping shapes, such as a circular mirror above a square sideboard or a mix of curved and straight-backed chairs, to introduce dynamic layering.

BALANCE OPPOSITES

Pair curved furniture, like a round coffee table, with more angular pieces, such as a rectangular sofa or shelving, to create contrast and harmony.

CREATE MOVEMENT

Arrange decor and furnishings to guide the eye. Layering rounded objects along a linear console or placing a curved lamp on boxy furniture can create a sense of flow.

TIPS AND TRICKS

01

TOO CLUTTERED?

Edit ruthlessly. Remove competing pieces to focus on adding balance and flow.

02

FLAT OR UNINSPIRED?

Add variety by using contrasting shapes, materials or heights to bring energy to the room.

03

DISCONNECTED LAYERS?

Tie elements together with repeated colours, materials or patterns across the space.

04

OVERWHELMED BY GREENERY?

Scale back and position the plants intentionally to anchor corners or frame views.

05

LACKING DEPTH?

Introduce overlapping elements, like rugs or textiles, to guide the eye and build dimension.

Layering transforms a room from ordinary to extraordinary. It's not about how much you add, but how you combine elements to create depth, balance and flow. Small tweaks can transform a chaotic space into one that feels harmonious and thoughtful. Every layer plays a part, from anchoring a room to softening its edges or creating movement. Thoughtful layering evolves over time, inviting exploration and adding richness to the design.

A well-layered space isn't just great to look at, it's wonderful to experience. It invites you to linger, notice the details and feel the harmony of elements working together. This balance of intention and personality is what makes layering essential to great design.

CRAFTED THROUGH TIME

In the labyrinthine heart of Marrakech's Medina lies a house with a soul woven from centuries. Riad Rosemary, built within one of the city's oldest neighbourhoods, feels like a living gallery. It is a canvas of design, craftsmanship and memory.

The story begins with Belgian architect Quentin Wilbaux, whose passion for preserving the riads of Marrakech – traditional Moroccan houses with enclosed gardens or courtyards – echoes through every restored detail. But this house is more than history. It is a celebration of what it means to layer the old with the new, the traditional with the playful.

At the centre of Riad Rosemary, a forty-year-old jacaranda tree stretches skyward, its canopy casting dappled shadows that ripple across hand-carved pillars and a tranquil courtyard pool. The walls, cloaked in dusty pink tadelakt, a traditional Moroccan clay-like plaster, are etched with delicate carvings, each line a conversation between artisan and imagination. Beneath your feet, a terrazzo floor tells a story of its own: squiggly and imperfect, its thousand-plus pieces were laid by hand to create a surface as textured as the city itself.

Everywhere you look, there are layers of craft and care. Stained glass scatters jewel-toned light into rooms that soar to heights of four metres. Modern embroidered linens and ceramic treasures, designed in-house by the Moroccan design studio LRNCE, lend a playful, personal touch. Even the wrought-iron handles on the doors feel alive, having been shaped by hands that understand both metal and poetry.

This is a home where time feels elastic. Every object, every detail, every brushstroke carries the weight of tradition but wears it lightly. Here, layers are not just physical, they are emotional, cultural and deeply human – testament to the beauty of living in harmony with history while dreaming of the future.

↖ PREVIOUS A hidden oasis tucked away in the heart of Marrakech, Riad Rosemary welcomes visitors into its handcrafted world of layers, culture and an artistic touch that could only belong to LRNCE.

←← ↓ Layers of handcrafted pieces, furniture, plinths, sculpture, plants and colour build a unique world in a city of tradition. The materials of history are all there, but the ways in which they are applied are new – Riad Rosemary tells its own story.

←↑ Every detail has a handmade touch, from the painted mosaics to the patterned zellige tiles. Patterns are layered upon colours, and the ever-present element of greenery softens the harder stone and ceramic surfaces.

The main living room of Riad Rosemary is a showcase of the signature LRNCE palette. Abstract patterned cushions and textiles create functional artworks across the long inbuilt sofa.

← An unexpected pop of chrome adds a layer of modernity to the traditional materiality of the space. Hand-carved chairs act as sculptures – form and function coming together in this artful space.

↑ Playing with the scale and textures of objects gives each room dramatic tension. These ideas should clash but instead come together to become a visually dynamic and interesting space.

← The riad is finished with tadelakt walls, a traditional Moroccan plastering technique known for its smooth, polished finish and water-resistant properties. It brings luxury to the space, but with a tactile rustic visual.

← ↑ The moment you step into any riad, the hustle and bustle outside the walls disappears and the world suddenly becomes quiet. At Riad Rosemary, you are also transported into a lush world of greenery with hidden pockets to escape to and rest in.

↑ ↗ The original structures of the building are still present, but they are overlaid with new forms that echo the past and bring modernity to traditional materials and shapes.

↑ In rooms where natural light is not abundant, Rosemary uses glass in the most unique ways. Creating artworks out of stained panels allows light from the bathroom to filter through the room, layering colours and shapes through this magical method.

→ A place where time holds its breath, where past and present intertwine, and where the indoors and out merge seamlessly. Every layer tells a story.

SIX

SPACE

SIX

Before you start cooking, you need a clean, well-organised space to work in. Without it, your flavours (or furniture) will get muddled, and the magic of the final dish will be lost. Great design, like great cooking, begins with allowing your ingredients to breathe. By embracing the beauty of simplicity and understanding the importance of balance, you can create spaces that feel open, intentional and alive with possibility.

‘Elegance is elimination.’

CRISTÓBAL BALENCIAGA · 1895–1972 · FASHION DESIGNER

Finding a Balance

I have always been drawn to the exuberance of maximalism – vivid colours, bold patterns, art covering every wall, and carefully curated collections arranged on every available surface. I believed I was someone who finds joy in vibrant chaos. Then I met my husband.

He is also a designer, but his aesthetic is the complete antithesis of mine. His ideal home would consist of a single concrete bench in an empty room. Well, maybe not quite that extreme, but his love for simplicity and restraint has made me reconsider my own approach to design. When we moved in together, I quickly learned that my maximalist instincts would have to evolve.

It wasn't an overnight transformation, more of a slow shift. I began to see the charm in a space with clean lines and room to move, and a home that felt calmer and more intentional. I still love colour and pattern, but now I know how to temper it, how to balance boldness with simplicity.

Space is not just the physical dimensions of a room, but the sense of openness and clarity that comes from thoughtful design. While I may not live as a minimalist, I have learned how to live with one. I have a new appreciation for the way that space – real, unencumbered space – can transform a home. By making the most of the space you have, you can create an environment that is both serene and full of life.

Let the details shine by allowing them to breathe. Restraint is sometimes the most important element of design.

Space isn't just the emptiness between objects, it's the foundation of thoughtful design. It shapes how we move, feel and interact within a room. By learning to observe the key characteristics of a space – including negative space – you can unlock the subtleties of balance, flow and purpose in any interior.

FOCUS FLOW NEGATIVE SPACE CONNECTION DETAIL

KEY CHARACTERISTICS OF SPACE

① FOCUS

What draws your attention first? Is there a clear focal point in the room or are there lots of elements competing for attention?

② FLOW

How does the room guide movement? Are there clear pathways? Is it easy to navigate without bumping into furniture or does it feel restricted?

③ NEGATIVE SPACE

Where does the eye rest? Are there moments of intentional emptiness to give objects room to breathe?

④ CONNECTION

Do the elements in the space feel connected? Is there a sense of cohesion or do some areas feel at odds with others?

⑤ DETAIL

What role do the architectural features play in shaping the room? Does the moulding, trim or the clean lines of the furnishings enhance the openness or add a subtle structure?

HOW TO CREATE BREATHING ROOM

REMOVE THREE ITEMS

If a room feels crowded, start by removing three small objects. Step back and assess the impact. This simple edit often makes the entire space feel more open and considered.

ROTATE DECOR

Not every piece has to be on display all the time. Rotate items seasonally or when inspiration strikes. By shifting elements, you will rediscover their charm and keep the space feeling fresh.

USE MULTI-FUNCTIONAL FURNITURE

Consider furniture that doubles as storage, like a sleek bench with hidden compartments. These pieces maintain the room's openness while helping keep clutter out of sight.

THE ROLE OF NEGATIVE SPACE

Negative spaces are the areas of a room that have been intentionally left blank. They act like a comfortable pause in a conversation. They let the eye rest, create balance and help individual elements stand out. For example, in a room with a striking armchair and a bold piece of art, a stretch of open floor between them ensures that each one can be appreciated without overwhelming the other. Leaving some areas unoccupied gives other areas, and pieces, a stage on which to shine.

FOCUS AND FLOW

A clear focal point helps to anchor a space, and ease of movement through a room ensures a sense of purpose and comfort. The focal point of a room could be a fireplace, a large window or a signature piece of furniture. Once you have identified what naturally draws the eye, you can arrange your layout to support it.

A space that feels off-balance is often an issue of proportion and scale. A large sectional sofa will dominate a small living room, making it feel cramped, just as a smaller loveseat will leave a larger room feeling sparse. Matching the scale of the furnishings to the size of the room ensures a more harmonious flow.

Finally, think about how people will move through the space. Well-planned flow not only makes a room functional but also helps to make it feel welcoming and calm.

WHEN LESS TRULY BECOMES MORE

Minimalism doesn't mean stripping away character or erasing personal touches. It's about distilling the essence of a room down to its most meaningful elements. A single vintage chest, a soft wool rug or a well-placed piece of art can evoke a sense of calm and focus. What's left is not just a functional space, but space that feels intentional. Every object has a purpose, and every absence feels like an invitation to breathe.

NOT ANOTHER WHITE BOX

Let's get one thing straight. Minimalism isn't just about throwing out your knick-knacks and painting everything stark white. I'm all for clean lines and open space, but I draw the line at feeling like I'm checking into a clinic every time I walk into a room.

A clutter-free life doesn't mean a colour-free life. Soft beiges, warm taupes, even a rich navy or a deep maroon can all thrive in a minimalist setting. They add warmth and character without tipping the scale back towards chaos. Minimalism can have texture, it can have depth, and yes, it can have colour. White walls might be a blank canvas, but there is a world of elegant, soothing hues waiting to be explored.

So let's retire the idea that minimalism means a flat, lifeless palette. Instead, think of it as a fresh start, a chance to embrace a few beautiful, considered tones that let the space feel calm, curated and – most importantly – inviting.

Embrace what you're working with. Raw walls and texture doesn't mean that a room isn't minimalist. These elements give the furniture a unique backdrop – no more needs to be added.

In a minimalist home, where fewer distractions compete for attention, architectural details can take centre stage. Instead of being hidden by layers of decor, they are celebrated, bringing quiet elegance and thoughtful craftsmanship to the forefront.

Clean, monochrome colour schemes serve as a neutral canvas, allowing the inherent beauty of the architecture to emerge. A subtle curve in an archway, the crisp line of a window frame or the intricate craftsmanship of moulding becomes a focal point that enriches the space.

By painting walls, ceilings and trims in a cohesive palette, the interplay of light and shadow across surfaces becomes more pronounced. These details, often overlooked in busier interiors, gain prominence, adding character and depth. A well-proportioned alcove, the texture of exposed brick, or the grain of wooden beams can take on a sculptural quality, turning the home itself into a work of art.

MIDIMALISM:
THE BEAUTY OF THE IN-BETWEEN

Not quite maximalist, not quite minimalist, midimalism lives comfortably in the middle, where there is just enough intentional curation to make a space feel complete without being overwhelmed. It's about paring back with purpose, but not so far that a space loses its warmth or individuality. Instead of a stark white room with a single chair, imagine a well-edited collection of ceramics on a shelf, a thoughtfully chosen rug anchoring the furniture, and a few textured cushions that add personality without tipping into clutter.

Midimalism is the best of both worlds: the clarity and calm of minimalism balanced with the character and charm of a more layered space. It's a design philosophy that encourages you to keep what matters, what feels right and what tells your story, while letting go of the unnecessary.

In a midimalist space, everything has its place and purpose. It's not about living with less or more, it's about living with what's just right. The objects you choose, be it a sleek table lamp, a vintage wooden stool or a cosy wool throw, become deliberate statements rather than background noise. Negative space is still present, but it feels intentional, not barren. The result is a home that is uncluttered, yet full of life.

↑ Careful curation and investments in key pieces makes design intentional – you can decide where you fall on the spectrum of maximalist to minimalist.

TIPS AND TRICKS

01

TOO CLUTTERED?

Remove three small items
or one large piece of furniture.
Notice how the room breathes anew,
as though it exhales.

02

TOO SPARSE?

Layer a rug, introduce a plant
or add a textured throw.
A hint of warmth can ignite
even the starkest corner.

Space, in the end, is much more than the absence of objects. It's the presence of possibility. It offers a canvas for light to wander, for stories to unfold and for life's small rituals to take centre stage. Embracing emptiness where it counts, and carefully considering where to place each treasured piece, creates a home that feels purposeful and serene. In that balance, every element, every furnishing, every memory finds its place and its voice.

A QUIET REVELATION

IN EAST LONDON'S HISTORIC HEART, this Georgian home, built in 1717, stands as a quiet ode to restraint. This is a house where simplicity doesn't strip away character, it amplifies it. Each space feels intentional, its beauty emerging not from excess but from the decision to let every detail breathe.

The home's transformation was an exercise in peeling back layers to reveal its integrity. Walls that were once crowded with pattern now carry a soft, cohesive palette, calming the eye and drawing focus to the craftsmanship of the past. Bare floorboards, their pale grain worn smooth by time, stretch through the house like a quiet echo of those who have walked here before.

Furnishings are sparse yet thoughtful. In the basement, a Shaker-style kitchen and antique chairs surround a long oak table. This is a place for gathering and connection. Upstairs, simple furnishings, from an aged timber table to a daybed softened with natural textiles, feel curated without pretension.

Even ornamentation has been reconsidered. A painted stormy sky lingers on the music room ceiling in a playful nod to the past, and reclaimed stone and climbing greenery make the courtyard garden a serene escape.

This is a house that holds its history lightly, letting its spaces breathe and its stories linger. It is a sanctuary of subtlety, where the power of space lies in its ability to distil life down to its essential elements.

↖ PREVIOUS Similar to the process of the restoration, where layers were peeled back to reveal history, this home's stunningly elegant simplicity is revealed around every corner.

← Light filters through the historic windows of this small sitting room. Dark accents keep the palette restrained and cohesive, and hints of timber and leather connect the space.

← ↑ The bedroom lets the architecture do the talking. Panelling on the walls guides the eye to the cornice, focusing on the simpler details rather than adding any more to the room.

↑ Colour blocking a mixture of vintage objects brings an organised visual to this vignette. It keeps the concept of minimalism through cohesion and colour without sacrificing the integrity of the objects themselves.

→ The bathrooms are kept simple, with no ornamental tiling to distract from the clawfoot tub. They offer a sense of calm and peace.

↑ The kitchen's Shaker-style cabinets by deVOL add deep accented tones against the pale walls. A baker's rack holds collected pieces that are in use every day, keeping the curation intentional.

← ↑ Vintage furniture is paired with clean modern lines, hinting at the history of the original home without adorning every corner. Nothing feels museum-like; every piece feels used, lived in and necessary.

axel vervoordt

The music room pulls a double act – feeling both minimal and comfortable at the same time. One doesn't need to cancel the other out – the choice of materials, textures and deep colours help to bring a cosy element to this space.

SEVEN

CULTURE

SEVEN

Culture in interiors is like a family recipe – full of history, personal touches and traditions that make it unique. Every ingredient has a story, just as every piece in your home reflects the places you've been and the influences that have shaped you.

'Travel isn't always pretty. It isn't always comfortable. Sometimes it hurts, it even breaks your heart. But that's okay. The journey changes you; it should change you.'

ANTHONY BOURDAIN · 1956–2018 · CHEF AND TRAVEL DOCUMENTARIAN

A World of Influence

I love the way that travel leaves an imprint on you. Every time I return home, I find myself seeing the familiar through a slightly different lens. Growing up with German grandparents and my mum's family in Taipei has shaped how I see the world. It has given me an appreciation for contrasts, traditions and the influence that different cultures have on one another. My partner, who loves scent, has taught me to notice the earthy aroma of eucalyptus in Tasmania, the faint sweetness of a tea ceremony in Taiwan and the spices wafting through a market halfway across the globe.

In Japan, I was struck by the quiet beauty of wabi-sabi minimalism, and its celebration of imperfection and simplicity. This inspired the handmade ceramic pieces I brought home and now eat off every night. Their raw, earthy textures and irregular shapes bring a sense of calm and imperfection to my table, reminding me of the ritual of dining I experienced in Japanese interiors.

Marrakech was a sensory feast of vibrant colours, intricate details and rich textures that made every corner feel alive. It has been translated into my home through a bold, abstract patterned rug with neutral and earthy tones that anchor the centre of my living room. It balances the more colourful hues of the space and provides a moment of art on the floor. The rug is a tactile reminder of the intricate handwoven textiles I encountered in the markets of Marrakech, and it brings an undeniable energy to the room.

Being influenced by travel or a cultural experience isn't about replicating it, it's about translating its essence in a way that feels natural to you. A muted palette, a hand-thrown ceramic vase or layered textiles inspired by travels aren't details that are overwhelming, but they will enrich a space.

Travel has taught me to approach design with curiosity and respect, weaving inspiration from different cultures into my work in ways that feel authentic and deeply personal. When done thoughtfully, cultural influences create spaces that are layered, meaningful and connected to the world.

Cultural influences in design are more than surface level decoration; they are about connection, history and meaning. It is important to embrace them with curiosity and respect. Learning the history of an item and sourcing authentic artisan pieces both adds depth to the role they play in a space and supports the communities behind them.

Understanding some key characteristics of culture and how they are used in design helps you create a space that resonates with meaning and purpose and builds a rich connection to the world around you.

CONNECTION CONTEXT AUTHENTICITY BALANCE RESPECT

KEY CHARACTERISTICS OF CULTURE

① CONNECTION

What draws you in? Is it the textures, the proportions or the colours? Can you identify the elements that feel personal and speak to your experiences?

② CONTEXT

How does it fit within your space? Does it complement the architecture or feel at home in its surroundings? Does it add focus to the room without overwhelming it?

③ AUTHENTICITY

Does it feel true to its origins, or exaggerated?

④ BALANCE

How do the different influences interact? Do they feel harmonious, or do they compete with each other?

⑤ RESPECT

Do you understand the significance of the object or decorative element? Are you honouring its story?

DISPLAYING CULTURE THOUGHTFULLY

Bringing elements of one culture into a different environment is a delicate dance. A distinctive piece may find its place in your home, but the design must consider the surrounding context and feel cohesive. The goal is to create a conversation between the elements, blending influences in a way that enhances rather than dominates. This balance can be achieved through restraint and intention. Incorporate cultural details as accents rather than dominant features. Subtle references, a palette, material or motif, often work better than recreating an entire aesthetic.

TRAVEL MEMORIES: CULTURE BEYOND DESIGN

Design is not the only way we absorb and carry culture home with us. It's also the experiences we gather, the plate of pasta eaten in a bustling piazza, the quiet ritual of a tea ceremony, or the feeling of warm sun on your skin as you sip a drink by the coast. These memories shape the way we view the world and infuse our lives with meaning long after the trip is over. They may influence how we approach cooking, hosting, or simply enjoying a quiet moment.

Incorporating these moments into your home is about more than just objects. It's about creating spaces that evoke the feelings you had during those experiences. A communal dining table may remind you of shared meals abroad, while a cosy corner with layered textiles might recall the warmth of hospitality. These are the details that transform a house into a living memoir, full of stories waiting to be told.

Layering cultural influences is about more than just mixing styles, it's about creating a cohesive dialogue between elements that resonate with you. Whether it's the craftsmanship of an artisan piece or the subtle echo of a colour palette, these layers should add depth and meaning without overwhelming the space. The aim is to let each piece tell its story while contributing to the broader narrative of your home.

HOW TO LAYER CULTURAL REFERENCES

START WITH ONE STRONG ELEMENT

Choose a key piece from a culture that inspires you and build your design around it to avoid visual clutter. Try situating bold pieces in understated surroundings to let them shine.

BLEND, DON'T OVERWHELM

Combine cultural influences subtly, creating contrast without clashing. Allow them to interact, enhancing the narrative without overloading the design.

FIND COMPLEMENTARY COLOURS

Use palettes that bridge cultural elements, ensuring harmony in the overall design.

FOCUS ON CRAFTSMANSHIP

Prioritise handmade or artisan pieces that reflect the authenticity of their culture, bringing both beauty and meaning to the space.

INCORPORATE NATURAL MATERIALS

Cultures often connect to their landscapes. Use natural textures to bring a tactile and grounded feeling to the design.

EVOLVE OVER TIME

Let your space grow as you gather new inspirations from your travels, creating a home that evolves with your experiences.

IT'S A SMALL WORLD (BUT LEAVE THE THEME PARK AT THE DOOR)

We've all been there – swept up in the magic of a trip, standing in a bustling market, enchanted by the colours, sounds and atmosphere. And then, you spot it. The souvenir you're convinced will bring the spirit of your travels home. But, once it's unpacked, that miniature Eiffel Tower or beaded camel figurine suddenly feels a little… off.

Incorporating cultural influences into your home doesn't mean creating a theme-park version of a city. Your space should feel inspired, not staged. Think less 'miniature gold gondola' and more 'Venetian glass sconce'. Find pieces that speak to the craft, beauty and essence of a place, rather than its clichés. By choosing items with intention and weaving them into your existing space, you create a home that feels worldly, meaningful and uniquely yours. Without even a whiff of 'tourist trap'.

HONOURING HERITAGE WITHIN MODERN DESIGN

Not only can cultural influences add depth, they can also be a way to honour personal or ancestral heritage. Incorporating elements of your own cultural identity can bring a profound sense of belonging to your space. Whether it's handmade ceramics, traditional textiles or a family heirloom, these pieces ensure that your home is not just inspired by the world but also grounded in your story.

Italian vases adorn shelves of a workshop in Puglia. My friend Claudio visited this small town and his own home now holds some of these pieces, bringing Italy back in a small way.

Using items in practical ways is a great way to incorporate a cultural story into a home. Japanese baskets act as wood storage, making a forgotten object of the home a story in itself.

That vintage plate that's been passed down through the family may not have a place on the table for you but it might find a new life as an artwork hanging on a wall.

Ceramics and pottery are great ways to incorporate cultural mementos and heritage into a space. They're practical, unique and can be used every day.

THE CULTURAL MEMORY OF FRAGRANCE

Scent is a powerful and often overlooked element in design, deeply tied to memory and emotion. It's said that scent is the strongest trigger of memory, capable of transporting us to specific places and moments. Incorporating scent into your home can evoke the essence of a culture or the memories of a journey, creating an invisible yet impactful layer in your space. Whether it's the aroma of spices that reminds you of a bustling market or the earthy scent of rain-soaked wood on a rainy day abroad, scent can tell a story and enhance the overall atmosphere of a room.

By thoughtfully integrating scent into your design, you can connect your home to the cultures that inspire you while making it a multi-sensory and memorable experience for anyone who enters.

HOW TO INCORPORATE SCENTS

CREATE LINKS TO PERSONAL MEMORIES

Select fragrances that remind you of meaningful experiences, like the fresh citrus from a Mediterranean trip or the woody aroma of an Eastern temple.

LAYER NATURAL ELEMENTS

Use fresh flowers, herbs or essential oils associated with the culture you're inspired by – lavender for a Provencale touch or sandalwood for an Indian influence.

CANDLES AND DIFFUSERS

Choose candles or diffusers crafted by artisans, with scents that are true to the region they represent. This ensures both quality and authenticity.

INCORPORATE FUNCTIONAL SCENTS

Bake bread, brew spiced tea or simmer herbs to fill your home with natural, cultural aromas that align with your lifestyle.

EXPERIMENT WITH INCENSE OR RESINS

For a more traditional approach, consider burning incense or aromatic resins linked to cultural practices, like frankincense or myrrh.

CONNECTIONS THROUGH MATERIAL AND CRAFT

Another way to integrate cultural influences is by sourcing materials and crafts directly from artisans. Handmade pieces carry the soul of their origin and ensure a connection to the culture that inspired them. A crafted basket or a hand-thrown vase brings not just beauty but a sense of authenticity and a direct link to its maker.

By layering these cultural connections into your home thoughtfully, you create a space that not only reflects your travels and inspirations but also respects the traditions that inspire it. A home influenced by the world is a home that feels exciting, and that will evolve with every new experience.

Culture enriches a home with depth and meaning by weaving together the memories, experiences and inspirations that shape who we are. It's not about recreating places but capturing their essence – the colours, scents and textures that stay with you long after the journey ends.

A home layered with culture is not just a reflection of where you've been, it is a celebration of how those moments have shaped the space you call your own.

A BRIDGE BETWEEN WORLDS

Tucked into the shadow of kunanyi/Mount Wellington, where Tasmania's wilderness meets the quiet hum of suburban life, Provider House stands as a testament to the beauty of cultural connection. This wooden cabin, hidden at the end of a dirt road in Lenah Valley, whispers of Japan – its simplicity, serenity and reverence for the everyday – yet remains firmly rooted in its Australian surroundings.

Provider House is not just a home, it is a story written in wood, scent and light. Every element has been carefully chosen, each detail infused with meaning. Tatami-like textures in woven furnishings, minimalist timber lines that nod to Japanese ryokans and hand-thrown ceramics that celebrate the artistry of imperfection all work together to create a space where culture is not only referenced but deeply felt.

Despite these influences, Provider House is distinctly Australian. The timber reflects the surrounding Tasmanian landscape, grounding the design in its local context. Mornings begin with light spilling softly over the mountains, illuminating the delicate grain of timber walls. The scent of wood smoke mingles with the earthy aroma of kindling gathered for the fire. And just as you begin to lose yourself in the Japanese influences, a glance outside brings you back to Tasmania. A wallaby pauses in the garden, its curious gaze framed by the window – a quiet reminder of the unique wilderness that surrounds this sanctuary.

Here, the Japanese ethos of shibumi – effortless grace – infuses every corner. Provider House bridges worlds, blending the essence of two places into a singular, deeply personal sanctuary. This is a home where culture is not borrowed but lived. A place to honour tradition while finding stillness at the edge of the world.

←↑ Mossy mounds tumble down a hill in the Tasmanian bush, arriving at this timber cabin. Step into another world, another culture and another sense of self.

JAPAN

← The kitchen overlooks lush bushland greenery. Collected pieces from Japan fill the drawers – ramen bowls, trivets, even a toaster oven. This home integrates the cultural sensibility of another country with ease.

↑→ The essence of Provider House is shibumi – a Japanese aesthetic concept that emphasises simple, understated beauty, and is often characterised by an elegant, natural and effortless quality.

← ↑ Hints of Japanese cultural influence are found in the maple tree in the corner of the room, and the paper lantern that hangs above the dining table. This isn't a traditional Japanese space, but the visual cues are there.

↑ → Western furniture mixes with Japanese materiality to bridge the gap between culture and design. Raw timbers and linens add a wabi-sabi sensibility to each room.

← ↑ When the Tasmanian weather inevitably knocks against the windows, a soak in the ryokan-inspired bathtub will transport you to a place and time far, far away.

EIGHT

STORY

EIGHT

In the end, your home is your signature dish. It might be a constantly changing work in progress that features collected treasures, or a perfectly curated space, but all that matters is that it's unmistakably yours. It's the one that only you can make.

'You can take the most ordinary thing,
and if you know how to tell the story, you can
make it seem magical.'

STEVIE NICKS · 1948– · SINGER-SONGWRITER

The Stories We Live in

When I moved into my first apartment on my own, I was eager to create a space that felt 'grown up'. I leaned heavily on the trends of the moment - minimalist, Scandi-inspired interiors were very popular at the time. My home was a well-executed imitation of what I thought 'good design' was: blush cushions, black-and-white accents, clean lines, a big fiddle leaf fig in a corner. It ticked all the right boxes and looked like it belonged on a Pinterest board. But something was missing. It felt hollow. It could have belonged to anyone.

What it lacked was me. There was no personal story, no connection to who I was or what I loved. At the time, I didn't have the confidence to trust my instincts. I felt as if I was designing my space for other people to see, not for me to live in. But as I started collecting art, introducing vintage pieces and leaning into design elements that once intimidated me, something shifted. My space began to reflect not just what I liked, but who I was.

Now, many years later, design has become a way to tell my story. When I travel, I bring back objects that spark memories. A film, a piece of music or even a walk through a market can inspire how I layer textures, curate colour or style a corner. Every piece in my home has meaning, and together, they create a narrative that is entirely mine.

Design isn't just about how a space looks, it's about how it feels, how it connects to you and the stories it tells. That's where the magic happens.

The true heart of a home lies in its stories. While design provides beauty and function, it's the personal narrative woven through these elements that gives a space warmth and authenticity. The items you choose to display – heirlooms, mementos or meaningful objects – can shape the mood, palette and atmosphere of your interiors.

Weaving stories into your interiors transforms your home into more than just a physical space. It becomes a living narrative, a reflection of who you are, where you have been, and the stories you are still writing.

PERSONAL HISTORY SENSE OF PLACE EMOTION INSPIRATION DEPTH

KEY CHARACTERISTICS OF STORY

① PERSONAL HISTORY

What does the space say about your experiences? Does anything remind you of meaningful moments in your life?

② SENSE OF PLACE

How does the space honour its surroundings? Does it reflect the architecture, history or landscape of its location? Does it feel as if it belongs in its environment?

③ EMOTION

What emotions does the space evoke? Joy, nostalgia, inspiration? Do the objects, colours and textures in the space spark the feelings you want to experience in your home?

④ INSPIRATION

What influences your design choices? What films, music, art or books resonate with you?

⑤ DEPTH

Does the space invite exploration? Could you layer unique finds, collections or meaningful details to add richness and encourage curiosity?

Story doesn't stop at decor; it can live in the bones of a building or what is outside the windows. Preserving original mouldings, exposing a brick wall that has been hidden for decades or restoring a vintage doorway can reveal chapters of a home's history. Heritage can speak through original floorboards or an antique fireplace that bridges eras. Embrace these features rather than concealing them. Their wear and tear carry authenticity and charm. You can also juxtapose historical architecture with contemporary furniture to create a dialogue across time. A sleek glass coffee table in a room with Victorian plaster cornices celebrates the evolution of style.

↑ Hidden above the pub at the Clarendon Arms Hotel in Evandale, Tasmania, are endless rooms that shape the story of this small Georgian village.

HOW TO ADD PERSONAL TOUCHES USING OBJECTS

Objects often transcend their decorative purpose, becoming tangible expressions of memory, heritage and personal passions that bring individuality and depth to a home.

FOUND OBJECTS AND SOUVENIRS

A pebble from a seaside trip, a small statue from an overseas flea market or a vintage camera discovered in a local thrift store can be a talisman reminding you of days past.

INHERITED TREASURES

Heirloom furniture or a collection of old family photos breathe lineage into a room, connecting the current residents with the stories of their ancestors. A threadbare quilt or a weathered trunk can be a portal to family history, resonating with quiet nostalgia.

REFLECTING PASSIONS

If you adore music, display your guitar or vintage records. A travel enthusiast might line a shelf with international postcards. These signs of passion transform interiors into self-portraits.

The natural landscape can inspire more than just materials, it can infuse a home with the colours, tones and mood of its surroundings. Imagine a home nestled in a forest, where deep greens and earthy browns echo the trees, and the dappled light of the canopy is reflected in soft, muted fabrics. In a coastal setting, the palette might shift to the weathered greys of driftwood, the soft blues of the sea and the creamy whites of foamy waves, evoking the calm and openness of the ocean. The influence of landscape extends to built environments – think of a city loft that reflects its urban roots with exposed steel beams and industrial lighting.

A home's narrative is shaped by its architecture, its history and its setting. Whether through preserving timeworn features, blending old and new, or reflecting the colours and textures of the landscape it is situated in, each layer adds depth and meaning, connecting the space to its past, its environment and its inhabitants.

INTERIORS INSPIRED BY FILM AND ART

On screen, production designers craft spaces that are not bound by practicality, but inspired by storytelling .This often results in grand, bold and emotionally evocative worlds. When thoughtfully adapted, these cinematic ideas can bring layers of personality and drama into your home.

Movies aren't just stories, they are visual feasts. The way they create worlds using colour, texture and setting is fascinating. They are like mood boards in motion – richly layered, meticulously curated and brimming with inspiration. Their interiors, landscapes and lighting hint at ways to craft spaces that feel as cinematic as they are personal.

Think of the pastel symmetry and whimsical charm of Wes Anderson's films, with their meticulously arranged frames, or the sleek, modernist penthouse in Christopher Nolan's *The Dark Knight*, with its clean lines and moody sophistication. Equally inspiring are the layered, storied homes of Nancy Meyers's heroines, which are brimming with warmth, texture and lived-in charm. They feel both aspirational and relatable.

Art offers a more grounded but equally transformative source of inspiration. The expansive, meditative quality of Mark Rothko's colour fields can be translated into a home through rich, uninterrupted backdrops that evoke emotion and depth. The power of Rothko's work lies in the way colour blocks create a contemplative atmosphere. This can be mirrored in a space through thoughtfully chosen tones that envelop the room, allowing the mood to shift and deepen. These serene, monochromatic moments can anchor a space, creating a feeling of calm that lets other elements breathe and come to the forefront.

Cézanne's pastoral landscapes, with their earthy tones and organic forms, inspire a different kind of design approach. These scenes can influence vignettes composed of vintage finds – a rustic wooden table adorned with ceramics, an antique armchair draped with a soft linen throw, or even handwoven rugs that echo the textures of the countryside. Cézanne's palette and subject matter also encourage the use of natural materials like stone, terracotta and weathered wood, which bring a sense of timelessness and connection to nature into a home.

A home can be both a canvas for artistic expression and a stage for cinematic storytelling. Together or apart, they offer endless possibilities for creating interiors filled with meaning and imagination.

THE ULTIMATE INTERIOR WATCHLIST

If I weren't an interior designer, I'd probably be working in film. Here is a short list of my favourites, each one offering a unique aesthetic to explore, adapt and make your own.

THE FALL (2006)

Known for its surreal, dreamlike visuals and bold use of colour, Tarsem's film offers inspiration through its rich tapestries, ornate settings, and exotic, fantastical locations that evoke a sense of wonder and opulence.

A SINGLE MAN (2009)

Tom Ford's debut is a masterclass in mid-century modern elegance. With its rich textures, warm tones and impeccably curated furnishings, this film provides a wealth of inspiration for those who love timeless, sophisticated interiors that balance form and function.

THE VIRGIN SUICIDES (1999)

Sofia Coppola's dreamy debut captures the suburban melancholy of the 1970s through soft, hazy lighting, pastel palettes and nostalgic decor that evokes a sense of longing and innocence.

CALL ME BY YOUR NAME (2017)

Luca Guadagnino's film celebrates the effortless charm of an Italian villa. Rustic terracotta floors, aged wood and antique furnishings are paired with sun-drenched rooms and lush outdoor spaces, inspiring interiors that blend old-world charm with relaxed, contemporary living.

FUNNY FACE (1957)

This Audrey Hepburn and Fred Astaire classic is a love letter to mid-century Parisian chic. From the minimalist elegance of a Parisian atelier to the vibrant colour pops of haute couture fashion shoots, its playful sophistication and refined aesthetic are inspiring.

IN THE MOOD FOR LOVE (2000)

Wong Kar-wai's masterpiece is a study in restrained elegance, with moody lighting, intimate spaces and rich jewel tones. The meticulous use of texture and vintage mid-century details make it an interior design dream.

HOW WE LIVE: STORIES OF SHARED MOMENTS

When thinking about how you can bring your personal story to your home, consider how you live in it. Your daily routines and shared moments with loved ones are part of its evolving story. The dining table where many laughter-filled dinners have unfolded, a cosy corner that holds the memories of quiet mornings with a book, and a well-worn sofa that tells of countless family movie nights. These lived experiences are the heartbeat of a home, transforming it from a curated space into a place alive with connection and meaning.

↑ My personal story sits with this place, Piermont in Swansea, Tasmania. This is where we held our wedding, where our friends and family came together, and those feelings (both mentally and physically) are what I try to capture in my own home.

Though a home can be admired for its aesthetics alone, it's the stories that give it soul. Every object, be it heirloom or newly crafted, whispers fragments of experience, weaving a tapestry that is intimately yours. As you live, grow and gather fresh memories, your home's story will keep evolving, reflecting each chapter of your shared journey. In this silent dialogue between past and present, the mundane transforms into the magical. Design, in its highest form, always holds space for our deepest connections and cherished tales.

ETCHED IN STONE AND SEA

THE BURROWS SITS QUIETLY on Tasmania's east coast, cradled by the rugged landscape and gazing out over Great Oyster Bay. Built in the 1860s, this cottage has weathered time with grace. Its stone walls and timber heart hold the stories of generations. Each addition, from the mid-century to today, has been layered with intention, preserving its spirit while weaving new tales into its foundation.

Inside, the home speaks in soft tones and collected treasures. Vintage furniture and salvaged finds tell of markets and makers, and handpicked artworks bring colour and texture to its quiet walls. The design is a narrative in itself – one that values the beauty of imperfection and honours the craftsmanship of the past.

The living room, with its plump feather sofa and a window seat framing Freycinet's rugged peaks, feels like a page left open, inviting moments of connection and calm. The bathhouse, with its clawfoot tub and leadlight French doors, is a chapter of indulgence, where the sunset casts its golden prose over the bay. Even the kitchen, stocked with local provisions, encourages slow meals that linger in a celebration of place and time.

The Burrows doesn't rush to tell its story. It offers space where you can listen to the wind rushing through the coastal trees, the whisper of the sea, and the history etched into its stone. Past and present blend seamlessly, creating a retreat that feels timeless, layered and alive with memory.

↖ PREVIOUS A warm light flickers on as the sun sets over the Hazards Ranges and The Burrows comes to life. It feels like coming home.

← The kitchen isn't just the clichéd heart of the home, it is the essential thoroughfare of daily life. It invites people to sit around the table and chat as their host cooks, and it also connects the entry to the rest of the house.

↓ The kitchen is the main entry point and thoroughfare of the home and it sets the tone of what's to come in other rooms. Hints of travels, flea markets and experiences fill the space.

↑ → There is nothing more magical than the morning light streaming through these glass doors as the steam rises from the bathhouse. A simple chandelier captures every ray of sunlight as they dance around the room.

↑ This dark and moody bedroom evokes warmth and comfort. You can see the layers of history in the paint that coats the walls, and the antique armoire that flanks the room.

→ Vintage photos create a miniature accent and layers of linen encourage you to sink into the bed, look out at the mountains and watch the world roll by.

← A home full of stories inspires curiosity. When did you get this? Where did this come from? Every item has a tale to tell, big or small.

↑ Sometimes an object that doesn't really make any sense is the missing piece that ties everything together. This vintage Murano glass Sputnik chandelier was made worlds away from the Tasmanian coast but it fits in perfectly at The Burrows.

↑→ A home isn't a gallery. A home is where people live. It shows the reality of everyday life. The shelves stacked with dishes, the artwork leaning on the mantle, the bricks charred by decades above the stove. Perfection is over-rated; stories and history shine here.

RURAL

←↑ A home like this inspires you to create your own stories. It might make you want to paint, get lost in books or start collecting objects you find in the natural world that surrounds it. Pause, take a moment, and find ways to bring these feelings home with you.

Wake up early and catch the sunrise. Let nature help shape the story of your home by bringing in the outside in any way you can. The perfect morning, in the perfect home.

DIGESTIVO

A Visual Feast: Ingredients That Make a Home began as an exploration of design but became something much deeper. It is a journey into how we discover our spaces, our instincts and ultimately ourselves. Every chapter, every home, every shared story is a lesson in how to create a life as layered and meaningful as the rooms we inhabit. As we reach the end, I find myself reflecting on what stays with us, long after the design is done.

In these pages, I have shared the basic ingredients: light, colour, pattern, texture, layers, space, culture and story. Now it's your turn. Take these tools and experiment with them. Design isn't about getting it perfect on the first try, it's about trusting yourself to craft something that feels authentic to you. Play with the ingredients and mix them in unexpected ways. Try, fail, adjust and create until you find your own style – your signature dish.

You might be wondering what my signature dish is. The truth is, I haven't created it yet. My dream home still lives in my imagination. It is a little shack on the coast of Tasmania, a place my husband and I can transform together. I picture timber panelling, a view out to water, textured tiles, warm stone, soft suedes and a collection of quirky vintage treasures that we will add to over time. It's not just the materials that will make it our dream home, it's the memories we will create there. Just like a wonderful meal, it's not just the ingredients that make it unforgettable. It is laughter, love and quiet moments that bring the magic.

This book is about more than design. It is about our connections to ourselves, to the people we share our spaces with and to the world around us. And now it's over to you. Design boldly, live fully and create a home that is a canvas for the life you are creating.

PHOTOGRAPHY AND DESIGN CREDITS

CHAPTER ONE · LIGHT

PROJECT: The Rental

DESIGN
Ellison Studios (@ellisonstudios)

PHOTOGRAPHY
Jacqui Turk (@jacqui_turk): pp. 14, 17, 30–41
Anson Smart (@smartanson): p. 28

CHAPTER TWO · COLOUR

PROJECT: Sun Ranch

DESIGN AND CURATION
Julia Ashwood and Jamie Blakey (@sunranch_byron)

ARCHITECTURE AND BUILD
Balanced Earth Architects (@balancedeartharchitects)

PHOTOGRAPHY
Jacqui Turk (@jacqui_turk): pp. 46, 64–83

CHAPTER THREE · PATTERN

PROJECT: Newport House

DESIGN AND STYLING
Jono Fleming (@jono.fleming) and Ryan McGregor

PHOTOGRAPHY
Nic Gossage (@nicgossage): pp. 88, 95, 104–119

CHAPTER FOUR · TEXTURE

PROJECT: Sonoma Barn

DESIGN
Hommeboys Interiors (@hommeboys)

PHOTOGRAPHY
Adam Potts (@adampottsphoto): pp. 124, 127, 141, 144–157
Bess Friday (@bessfriday): pp. 142–143
Eileen Roche (@eileenmroche): pp. 158–159

CHAPTER FIVE · LAYERS

PROJECT: Rosemary Riad

DESIGN
Laurence Leenaert, LRNCE (@rosemarymarrakech @LRNCE)

PHOTOGRAPHY
Marina Denisova (@_marinadenisova_): pp. 164, 176, 180, 184, 185, 191–197, 205
Jono Fleming (@jono.fleming): pp. 176, 182–183, 185, 188–189

CHAPTER SIX · SPACE

PROJECT: Stepney Townhouse

DESIGN
Paul West and Michelle Bower-West (@consideredthings)

PHOTOGRAPHY
Ellen Hancock (@ellen.christina.hancock): pp. 202, 214, 217–231
Paul West: p. 229

CHAPTER SEVEN · CULTURE

PROJECT: Provider House

DESIGN
Tara Bennett, TRIAS (@providerhousehobart)

PHOTOGRAPHY
Nic Gossage (@nicgossage): pp. 236–239, 246–249, 252–265

CHAPTER EIGHT · STORY

PROJECT: The Burrows

DESIGN
Bek Burrows and Paul DeRuyter (@the_burrows_swansea)

PHOTOGRAPHY
Nic Gossage (@nicgossage): pp. 268–273, 284–299

STILL LIFE AND ADDITIONAL INTERIORS PHOTOGRAPHY

Nic Gossage (@nicgossage) for *A Visual Feast*: pp. 2, 18–19, 25, 44, 50–51, 52, 53, 54, 55, 56, 63, 92–93, 96, 98–99, 101, 128–129, 139, 168–169, 206–207, 240–241, 248, 274–275, 280–281, inside back cover

Jacqui Turk (@jacqui_turk) for *A Visual Feast*: cover and pp. 6, 8, 9, 21, 22, 27, 60, 61, 62, 166–167, 171, 177, 204, 209, 215, 251

ADDITIONAL CREDITS

JONO FLEMING
pp. 244, 247, 248, 250

NIC GOSSAGE
pp. 200, 211, 212, 276–279, 282–283
for Inartisan: pp. 86, 126, 135
for Jono Fleming – design and styling by Jono Fleming: pp. 20, 100, 103, 136, 174; design by Jono Fleming and Allison Williams: p. 130
for Slow Beam – design by Hearth Studio and Lauren Bamford: p. 48

CAITLIN MILLS
for The Design Files – design by Jono Fleming, Strutt Studios: pp. 90–91

JESSIE PRINCE
for Inartisan: pp. 12, 162

LUCY STEVENS
pp. 49, 234, 242–243, 246

JACQUI TURK
for Inartisan: pp. 122, 131
for Studio Pulp – design by Studio Pulp, styling by Jono Fleming: pp. 172–173, 179, 213

KRISTIAN VAN DER BEEK
for Marz Designs: p. 16

LOUISE WELLINGTON
for The Design Files – design by Studio Esteta, JUMBLED: p. 58

THE LAST BITE

If I could set the table for the perfect dinner party, this would be the guest list. The people who brought ideas to the table, who stirred the pot with me, who added their own ingredients to make something greater than the sum of its parts. The ones who nourished me – creatively, emotionally, and quite literally – through every step of this process.

Ryan, my partner in life and design, my sounding board, my calm in the chaos – this book, like everything I do, is better because of you. The one who listens, refines, supports, and somehow makes everything better.

I couldn't have done this without *Jacqui Turk* and *Nic Gossage* – my work wife and husband – whose photography doesn't just capture spaces but brings them to life. More than collaborators, they have become family, the kind that comes with road trips, late-night wines, spontaneous spa days and the creative alchemy that only happens when people just get each other.

Paul McNally, who trusted me to run with this idea and let it be what it needed to be. Every book needs someone who says, 'Go for it!' Thank you for being that person.

Every tiny design decision, every page, every placement – it all came together because of *Susan Le*, who sat beside me through the details and the deadlines. Her patience, precision and talent made this book what it is. Let's go for laksa to celebrate.

Some people have a way of untangling your thoughts and making them clearer than you ever could on your own – *Lorna Hendry* is one of those people. Thank you for shaping these words with me.

The trajectory of my career changed the day *Claire Bradley* cracked open a door and let me step through. Having my family farm on the cover of *Inside Out* was a moment I'll always treasure, but the bigger gift has been the friendship that has lasted longer than magazines. For your generosity, laughter and belief in me, and for all those home-cooked meals and heartfelt chats in your apartment over the years – thank you.

Silvia Colloca, for reminding me that I don't have to pick just one lane – for showing me that I can do all the things I love. For all the time spent cooking together, sharing ideas and dreaming up new things. And to you and Richard, for trusting Ryan and me with your home, a place that now holds so much of our shared creativity and friendship. It's an honour to see it in these pages.

Some friendships are a foundation, a place to land no matter what. *Leeroy Morgan* and *Daisy Maung* are just that – my constants, my compass points. The ones who show up, who make ideas better, who make life funnier. Lee, this book wouldn't even have a title without you. I don't know what I'd do without you both.

There is no one more brutally (but beautifully) honest than *Lucy Stevens,* my soul sister and creative confidante. You keep me in check, and I wouldn't have it any other way. I will always answer on the first ring for you.

Scott Henderson, my biggest cheerleader – through every chapter of life, your advice and relentless positivity could have given me an overinflated ego, but instead, they gave me the confidence to pull this off.

Leigh McKeown, the one who listens to my wildest ideas and never lets me get away with half-baked ones. For keeping me honest and hearing me out – thank you.

A moment for the patient and kind *Bek Burrows,* for letting me share your home and Swansea with the world – the place where I got married, where so many memories live, and where a part of my heart will always belong.

Few things have inspired me more than the way *Laurence Leenaert* sees the world. Her art, her ceramics, her way of layering colour and texture – it has all shaped the way I think about design. Meeting her in 2018 in Morocco was a dream, and returning each year to stay at the beautiful Riad Rosemary is pure joy.

To those who let me share their spaces in this book – *Tara Bennett, Austin Carrier* and *Alex Mutter-Rottmayer, Julia Ashwood* and *Paul West* and *Michelle Bower-West* – your generosity has made these pages richer.

To *Karin Huchatz, Emily Heysen, Ray + Joe, Elise Pioch Balzac, Coco Reynolds, Kaety Thompson* and *Hali Rugs* – your images and objects don't just fill these pages, they fill my life.

And finally, my family – *Tracy, Pete, Chuck* and *Obi.* For your patience, your support, and for always being my greatest home.

A good dinner party lingers. The laughter, the stories, the way the night stretches longer than planned because no one wants to leave. This book is no different. It exists because of the people around this table, those who brought the best ideas, the sharpest insights, the unexpected twists, and the warmth that stays long after the last page is turned. I am endlessly grateful.

Smith Street Books

Published in 2025 by Smith Street Books
Naarm (Melbourne) | Australia
smithstreetbooks.com

Distributed outside of ANZ,
North & Latin America by
Thames & Hudson Ltd.,
6-24 Britannia Street, London, WC1X 9JD
thamesandhudson.com

EU Authorised Representative: Interart S.A.R.L.
19 rue Charles Auray, 93500 Pantin, Paris, France
productsafety@thameshudson.co.uk; www.interart.fr

ISBN: 978-1-9232-3941-8

Smith Street Books respectfully acknowledges the Wurundjeri People of the Kulin Nation, who are the Traditional Owners of the land on which we work, and we pay our respects to their Elders past and present.

PUBLISHER: Paul McNally
DESIGNER: Susan Le
EDITOR: Lorna Hendry
PROOFREADER: Pam Dunne
PRODUCTION MANAGER: Aisling Coughlan

Printed & bound in China by C&C Offset Printing Co., Ltd.

Book 410
10 9 8 7 6 5 4 3 2 1

FSC
www.fsc.org
MIX
Paper | Supporting responsible forestry
FSC® C008047